C000163547

Reef-fin's Saltwater Aquarium Guide for Beginners

How to Set Up a Marine Reef Aquarium for Fish and Corals, A Simple Step by Step Guide!

By,

Scott W. Fletcher

1

Text Copyright © 2020 by Scott W. Fletcher

All Rights Reserved.

Copyright© 2020 by Scott W. Fletcher

No part of this publication may be reproduced or transmitted in any form or by any means, or transmitted electronically without direct written permission in writing from the author.

This book was published with the intent to provide accurate information. While every precaution has been taken in preparation of this book, the author assumes no responsibility for error or omissions. Neither is any liability assumed for damages resulting from the use of this information herein.

The reader is fully responsible for their own actions.

All rights reserved.

Acknowledgements

My Dad,

Without your help and encouragement I would never have ventured into the hobby, so thank you. Who would have thought that our first freshwater fish tank would have led me down this path. This book and Reef-fin as a whole might never have happened if it wasn't for you taking your son to a fish shop on the weekends.

'Looks like we have cracked it'

My Dani,

For putting up with my obsession and being a crucial part of my hobby! Without your support in the hobby I may not be where I am today.

Myself,

For most of my adult life I have struggled with mild dyslexia (so I apologise in advance for any spelling mistakes, grammatical errors or poor punctuation). Writing this book has been challenging and time consuming. Although the book may not be perfect, it still remains a personal achievement. One I am constantly adding to and improving!

Table of Contents

Hello and welcome to...

The Reef-fin Guide,
A Beginner's Step by Step Guide to Setting Up A Saltwater Aquarium.

I will be as honest as I can be and share my many mistakes so you don't make the same ones! You really can have the aquarium of your dreams! It just takes a little bit of work.

First of all if at any time throughout this book you struggle to understand any aspect or you feel like you need to simply ask a question, please feel free to contact me via reef-fin's social media!!!

Sometimes having a chat can help put right any misunderstandings you have and can help clarify any aspect of this guide in a casual manor!

If you need more information on any aspect or simply need some more guidance then feel free to email!

Facebook –
https://www.facebook.com/reeffin.AquariumGuide/

Instagram – https://www.instagram.com/reef_fin/

You are about to enter one of the most rewarding hobbies I know of. Of course it has its ups and downs but there is nothing better than to sit back and simply admire your little piece of the ocean.

Honestly, I spend more time watching my reef tank than I do the TV.

You will meet so many great people within this hobby. Everyone I have spoken to over the years have been so friendly and helpful, I'm sure you will come to think the same.

If you use social media (such as Facebook) I recommend you join some local saltwater aquarium groups and get to know some of your fellow hobbyists. These groups are relatively good at answering those 'silly questions' and talking to fellow hobbyists can be a great way to learn about the hobby.

If you do not use social media then spend some time at your local fish stores and get to know some of your fellow hobbyists. Most people in this hobby love to chat about their aquariums!

This book is written under the impression you are a beginner and have a very basic understanding about the saltwater aquarium hobby.

If you have a good understanding of the hobby and are able to keep an aquarium up and running then I doubt this book is for you. It's still worth a read but you may not benefit in the way a beginner will.

I learnt something about the hobby from simply writing this book, so it does contain some useful information.

Before we get into the details of this book, you are probably wondering what Reef-fin is? And why you should listen/trust the information within this guide?

Any idiot who can read and type can publish a book, why should you trust what I have to say?

Well...

Here at Reef-fin I try to simplify every aspect of keeping a saltwater aquarium so that anyone can understand and follow my guidance. I don't miss out the important facts; I simple break them down and word them in a manner that anyone can follow.

Reef-fin is a marine aquarium blog that offers help, information and support to people who are just starting out in the hobby. My aim is to help you eliminate the 'trial and error' aspect of the hobby (which is costly in both time and money) and to offer you a chance to learn from my mistakes (and the mistakes of others) so you don't make the same ones.

Reef-fin must be doing something right as we have just made it into FeedSpots 'Top 30 Aquarium Blog Sites' list. Thank you again for everyone who voted for us!

I am well aware that some of the information on Reef-fin (and within this guide) can be found on the internet somewhere by a simple Google search. Unfortunately this can become overwhelming to the beginner as there can be a lot of conflicting information and a lot of scientific terminology out there. The combination of the above and the vast amount of opinions that are 'always correct' because it 'works in my tank' make setting up your first aquarium a very confusing process.

The purpose of this guide is to take all that information, combine it with those many ideas and opinions and order/ explain them in a manner anyone can follow.

Trust Reef-fin Yet?

Well like I said above, if any idiot can write a book, surely any idiot can make a blog?

So how do you know, that I know what I'm talking about?

Well this brings us round to the man who created reef-fin and that's me!

And by me, I mean Scotty.

I have kept saltwater aquariums for as long as I can remember.

I have kept many aquariums over the years and they have all varied in size and shape, from predator fish only to a mixed coral reef.

Now it's not the fact I am an expert in reef keeping that makes Reef-fin so popular among beginners. It's the fact I was once a clueless beginner who made every mistake possible though my early years of keeping a saltwater aquarium. Mistakes from rushing the cycling process to having too many fish, from forgetting about evaporation to over feeding. You name the mistake I probably made it at some point and then I probably made it again a few weeks later due to my lack of patience. It's safe to say I learnt the hard, long and very expensive way.

It's the combination of the above and my skills as a qualified teacher that have allowed me to write this book in a manner that others can learn from. The problem with many marine experts is not with their knowledge (as it's normally fantastic) but in the way they express that knowledge. My teaching background means I can take that knowledge and break it down into bite size chunks that anyone, from any background, of any age can follow.

My goal here is not to create the perfect book in terms of literature and writing style but to create a resource that is genuinely helpful to those who are just starting to create a saltwater aquarium. I can ramble on about aquariums, fish and corals all day but writing a book has proven challenging due to my personal difficulties (dyslexia). So please give this book a chance, the information is accurate but the grammar may not be perfect.

My aim is that this book will be a useful resource that will help guide you on your journey.

So if you are reading this then I am assuming you are willing to give this book a go? Good call as I believe this guide will help!

...and thank you ☺

So Let's Begin...

Anyone can have a successful saltwater aquarium. All it takes is some knowledge, a little bit of hard work and a few pennies. Oh, and a lot of patience!

Most people have this idea that a saltwater aquarium is going to break the bank because it's such an expensive hobby. Well that simply isn't the case. Yes that might have been true 30+ years ago when the hobby was in its infancy but as technology and our knowledge and understanding of the hobby has advanced, the hobby has become more accessible and manageable for the average person. It might cost more than a basic freshwater aquarium but probably no more money than a lot of other hobbies. This hobby is as expensive as you want it to be.

The amount of money you spend really comes down to what type of aquarium you are wanting.

Just remember to be realistic. Those beautiful coral reef aquariums you have seen on Google that are full of life and colour don't just instantly happen overnight. I take it you have heard of the saying Rome wasn't built in a day? Well it's the same for a saltwater aquarium.

(For The Beginner – This section will appear throughout this guide at the end of most chapters. This section is simply what I would recommend for the beginner. I will use this area to clarify aspects of the hobby and to give you my advice.)

Anyone can create a beautiful aquarium; you just have to know where to start...

Step 1a

First of All, What Do You Want?

Before you go out and randomly buy an aquarium you need to decide on a few things;

- What size aquarium you want?

- What type of aquarium do you want to keep?

- What livestock do you want?

- How much money can you afford to spend?

These four factors influence the entire hobby in some way, shape or form.

For example;

A large coral reef aquarium full of SPS corals (those hard looking corals, I will explain what they are later on) and many fish will cost a lot more money than a Nano fish only aquarium. A full reef aquarium will also have a bigger impact on your electricity bill. If you are on a small budget then a large reef aquarium may not be the best option.

So think about each of the four questions as you make your way through this book.

I have broken each one down to give you some idea of what is out there.

For more ideas why not scroll though Google, search the web and visit your local fish stores (LFS). Just have a look around and see what type of aquarium suits you and your needs.

This is a great opportunity to get to know your local fish stores and what the owners are like. Talk to them about your interest in the hobby and what you are wanting. You can normally tell the difference between a shop owner who is trying to help you and one that simply wants to make a sale. Finding a good LFS can make a huge difference and make your time in the hobby so much easier!

What Size Aquarium Do You Want?

Large Aquariums

Size isn't everything when it comes to a saltwater aquarium but sometimes bigger is better.

Starting out with a bigger aquarium is one thing many hobbyists wished they did. Most hobbyists, including myself, started off with a small aquarium and a few months later ended up getting a bigger one! I have upgraded the size of my aquarium four times in the past few years for no other reason than I needed more space. This hobby is great but you can get carried away.

Many hobbyists recommend going as big as you can when getting your first aquarium as a bigger aquarium can house more/ bigger fish. They also tend to be easier when it comes to keeping water parameters stable and here is why;

Imagine if a large glass of water and a shot glass of water were to represent two aquariums.

If you take some concentrated juice (this will be our nitrate, ammonia and other toxic parameters) and pour the same amount of juice in each glass, the shot glass will be a stronger drink. It would take a lot more juice in the bigger glass to make it as strong as the shot glass.

With me so far?

Well it's the same for our aquariums. It will take less nitrates (juice) to reach dangerous levels in a Nano aquarium (shot glass) than it will to reach dangerous levels in a large aquarium (Large glass). It's for this reason many experts believe a larger aquarium is more forgiving to mistakes and therefore better suited to the beginner.

However, there are two main draw backs to a larger aquarium, cost and space. If you live in a flat or a small home then a large aquarium isn't a sensible option. A larger aquarium will also cost more as you will need more equipment, more salt, bigger/more lighting units etc. So if you are on a small budget bigger might not be better.

Thankfully my partner is on board with my 'obsession' and does not mind my aquarium living in the front room. I know many hobbyists whose partners/ families are not too keen on them having a large aquarium in their home. So if you are going big, always inform the people you live with.

Obviously you would, right? I have seen many systems for sale as the hobbyist didn't inform their wife/husband on the size and had to sell. I'm not saying this applies to you, but it will apply to someone who simply gets carried away. I only mention it as I have seen it happen.

If a large aquarium isn't an option, then a smaller one might be better.

The Nano Aquarium

A Nano saltwater aquarium is just another word for a small aquarium of around 150 litres or less. Many beginners start off with a small aquarium as it seems like a 'safer' option but this isn't always the case.

Nano aquariums can be challenging and restricting not just for the beginner but for experienced hobbyists alike. Keeping parameters stable (as previously discussed) can often be challenging when dealing with a smaller volume of water.

You tend to be limited to the amount of livestock you can keep as there are only a small amount of fish that can be happily housed in a small aquarium. The fish you can keep in a small aquarium are normally labelled 'Nano fish' in most LFS or websites.

I personally love a Nano aquarium and have kept them for years. They are generally cheaper to run/fill and are ideal for smaller bedrooms and flats. If you simply want a pair of clownfish and a few corals then a Nano aquarium is ideal. Clownfish are hardy and relatively cheap fish that are perfect for the beginner. This is ideal as most people who want a saltwater aquarium want a pair of clownfish (aka. Nemo). So if clownfish are your reason for entering the hobby (because you 'want to have a Nemo fish') then a Nano aquarium will work for you.

TIP - When you are doing your research and getting to know people in the hobby you may come across the term 'Pico Tank'.

This is just another word for a very small Nano tank of around 25 litres or less. They look good but they are not for the beginner! This 'Tip' is merely an FYI to inform you of what one is in case you come across the term and wonder what it means.

No matter the size of an aquarium, what you are going to put in the aquarium also has a huge impact on the path you take in this hobby.

For the Beginner – I would recommend you start off with an aquarium of around 50 - 150 litres. Although this is still considered a small size for an aquarium within the saltwater hobby this size is very manageable. It's not too big that it will cost a fortune to fill and run but it's big enough that you can still keep a wide range of livestock. The shape of the aquarium doesn't really make a huge difference but you do want to aim for an aquarium that is longer than it is high. A tall aquarium isn't ideal for most marine livestock so a long shallow aquarium is what you should be looking for. For example; the fluval evo 13g is one I keep and it falls within these requirements. It's a reliable and cheap way to get into the hobby!

What Type Of Aquarium Do You Want To Keep?

There are several types of saltwater aquariums that are commonly kept in the home environment and all have their own unique benefits and restrictions. Most of the time it comes down to personal preference as to what type of aquarium you decide to set up.

Fish Only with live Rock or Fish Only Aquariums

Many fish, such as butterfly and angel fish will naturally eat coral. A fish only system is often the only way to successful keep many species of fish like this. You could keep them in a reef but why would you want to pay so much on corals for your fish to eat them? There are much cheaper methods of feeding your fish!

There are two main types of fish only aquariums, a predator and a communal aquarium. Predator tanks tend to house more aggressive fish such as triggers, lion fish, eels and puffers. Communal tanks will house your more peaceful fish.

Fish only systems tend to be easier to keep. It tends to be coral that are harder to keep within an aquarium. Fish tend to be resilient and more forgiving than many corals making them an easier option for many.

These aquariums can be of any size and are normally filled with aquarium décor such as sunken ships, fake plants, fake corals or the use of live rock.

Reef Aquariums

Probably the most expensive, difficult and most desired style of saltwater aquariums are the coral reef aquariums. They consist of soft corals (more suited for beginners), LPS corals or SPS corals and a mixture of reef safe fish and inverts. The goal here is to recreate the natural ecosystem found in our oceans.

Reef aquariums tend to need the most equipment and often to cost the most to run. A reef tank can be kept in any size aquarium as long as your water parameters are kept stable. Corals are delicate creatures and a swing in water parameters can cause them to become stressed and potentially die. It's for this reason reef aquariums are considered one of the more challenging types to keep.

I will go into more detail on corals, water parameters and fish later on.

For the Beginner – I would recommend you simply start off with a pair of clownfish and go from there. If you want to keep corals then add them at a later date once your aquarium is mature and established. At this stage what type of aquarium you are wanting doesn't make a huge difference as your aquarium will be somewhat bare to begin with.

No matter what type of aquarium you create, your ultimate aim is to keep livestock.

What Livestock Do You Want?

This links directly with what type and size aquarium you are wanting. A Bigger aquarium means bigger fish and a Smaller aquarium means smaller fish, simple really.

Just be sensible with what fish you choose. If you want a predator like a lion fish then you shouldn't be keeping them with smaller fish like Chromis, as the lion will naturally predate them. Do not try to change how a species will behave. Some fish are predators and some are territorial. Try to create an aquarium to suit the behaviour of the fish and you will have success. If you try to go against the nature of the livestock you keep you will never be successful. This is where research plays a huge role. Learn as much as you can about the livestock you want to keep and how to keep them. This may take longer but it's the best method for success.

Whatever fish you want to keep make sure you do some research on them to find out what type of aquarium they are best suited to. You will soon come to find that research plays a huge role in the preparation of building your aquarium.

If you are wanting corals then some fish are simply a 'no no' as they naturally feed on them. Fish that work well in a reef tank are normally labelled 'reef safe'.

In reading this book I am assuming you have already seen a fish that you want to keep. This is normally the reason for people wanting to set up a saltwater aquarium in the first place. If this is the case then you will already have an idea on the type of aquarium you want.

For the Beginner – I would fully recommend you start off with a pair of clownfish. Most clownfish are now captive breed so there is no impact on the wild population. These clownfish are resilient and adapt well to life in an aquarium making them ideal for the beginner.

If you can keep a pair of clownfish alive then you will be able to keep most fish suitable for a beginner. Clownfish are in high demand so if you don't want them long term your Local fish store will often take them off your hands. This tends to apply to those who want to keep a predator style aquarium as clownfish will do well in both fish only and coral reef aquarium.

Depending on where you are located will ultimately decide what your local fish stores will stock. Different stores around the world stock and keep different types of livestock. What you keep often comes down to what you can get. So try to visit several shops to get an idea of what fish are available in your area. This will give you an idea of what livestock you like and what size aquarium you will need to house the ones you want.

No matter what you decide to keep you are going to need some pennies.

How Much Money Can You Afford To Spend?

This is what normally puts people off getting into this hobby. Everyone has heard how expensive it is to keep a saltwater aquarium. This is and isn't true. This hobby is as expensive as you want it to be providing you are being realistic.

If all you want is a pair of clownfish in a Nano aquarium then you aren't going to have to spend very much. You could even get a few soft corals and it would still be relatively inexpensive.

However if you are wanting a large reef aquarium full of bright corals and fish then you may need a small bank loan (I might be exaggerating a little here when I say bank loan, but it isn't cheap) as equipment and livestock costs can soon add up.

I personally settled in the middle. I keep a Nano mixed reef tank that is relatively inexpensive and affordable on the average wage.

For the Beginner – An aquarium of around 50 – 150 litres should work well for the beginner. This will be the safer and cheaper option. The monthly cost of an aquarium for this size isn't unreasonable and the initial cost is generally no more than a new TV. An aquarium this size with some clownfish will give you a good starting point in the hobby.

If money is an issue have you thought about a second hand aquarium? Many Hobbyists sell full set ups in great condition on a regular basis. Try having a look on Ebay or other selling platforms to see what aquariums are for sale. Many of my systems have been second hand because, well, why not? Full saltwater aquarium set ups are not cheap and when hobbyists are selling these for half the price, I class this as a win!

Once you have your answer to each of the four questions (that I asked you earlier in this book) you will have a rough idea of what type of aquarium you are wanting.

Before you make any concrete decisions you need to figure out where you are going to put this aquarium?

1b

Aquarium Placement

Seems like an obvious thing to discuss but so many inexperienced hobbyists get this part wrong.

You need to think about where you want to put your aquarium now, as moving an aquarium full of rock and water simply isn't going to happen.

Below are a few things to consider when picking a place for your aquarium to live;

Keep Your Aquarium Out of Direct Sunlight.

You want to avoid placing your aquarium in a window or in direct sunlight for two main reasons.

First of all, if the sun hits your aquarium all day your water temperature is going to rise. This can be disastrous to all your livestock as temperature spikes can lead to a full aquarium crash.

Secondly, more light hitting your reef aquarium can often promote algae growth on the glass wall. While most algae blooms won't wipe out your aquarium they are annoying to remove and are often very unsightly.

Try to Avoid Putting the Aquarium in a Room Where You Won't See it.

I have done this in the past and placed the aquarium in a spare room. I spent so much time and money on my aquarium that I rarely appreciated it because I didn't see it often. As a result of this my maintenance took a hit and as the saying goes 'out of sight out of mind'. I didn't see the problems so I didn't fix them. Parameters started to swing, algae started to grow and livestock started to die. This 'out of sight' aquarium didn't last long before I broke it down and moved it to the kitchen which is a room we are always in.

Do not Place the Aquarium in a Busy Part of the Home.

By 'busy' I mean in a hall way where people are constantly walking past as the aquarium itself might get knocked and potentially damaged. Repeated stress to the walls of the aquarium overtime can cause leaking and structural failure. Small scratches become small cracks that become major leaks!

Do not Place the Aquarium near a Heat Source such as a Radiator or Air Conditioning Unit.

Although we use heaters and chillers in our aquariums some outside sources can have a dramatic affect on the temperature of your aquarium. This is not what you want when you are aiming for stability.

Aquarium Weight.

If you want you keep your aquarium upstairs then you need to make sure that the flooring can support the weight. When you combine the weight of water, rocks, sand, equipment and the tank itself, well let's just say it isn't light.

Power.

This is something I totally forgot about. Our Aquariums are not run on fairy dust (unfortunately) so when placing your aquarium make sure it is near a power supply or plug socket as having power cords running across a room isn't ideal. I had my first system filled to the brim with water when I realised there was no plug socket in sight. Like I said, I made a lot of mistakes in my youth, mainly down to a lack of planning and patience.

For the Beginner - The ideal tank placement (in my opinion) is somewhere you often relax or in a room where you spend a lot of time and can appreciate your aquarium. You want to avoid windows and walk ways and ideally place the tank near its own plug sockets. I have one in my bedroom and one in the living room. Both aquariums are seen often as I am always in one of them two rooms. Thinking about it I really should have one in the kitchen too...

For some people space can be a real issue but for others it's no problem at all. Each home aquarium is different and it will be the same for yours.

So before you move onto step 2 spend some time thinking about what type of aquarium you want and where you are going to keep it.

Step 2a

Filtration

Our fish, inverts and corals sleep, eat, play and poop (for lack of a better word) in the aquariums they live in. Over time this waste builds up and needs to be removed. If waste is left to build up in the aquarium the concentrations will rise to dangers levels where it can be lethal to most livestock.

Think about it, if we were locked in a house we would need a toilet that flushed! If not our waste would build up. We might get ill from the build-up of waste, disease from the parasites and bacteria living on the waste and it would generally be an unpleasant place to live. It's the same for the fish but they don't have a toilet like we do. So what do we do?

Well...

A mature saltwater aquarium will have a range of methods for removing waste from within the aquariums water column (skimmers, refugiums, filter socks, activated carbon etc.). These methods will generally filter the water to keep it clean in one of three ways; Mechanical, Chemical and Biological Filtration.

Mechanical Filtration

A mechanical filter takes particles out of the water to keep the water clear. They remove unsightly particles including fish excrement, sludge, uneaten food, or dust. To prevent all this waste building up, the filter media must be cleaned on a regular basis.

The components of mechanical filter media are inert which means they will do nothing to interfere with your water chemistry.

The most common type of mechanical filtration within a reef aquarium is the use of filter socks or roller mats (if you have a sump) or mesh inserts and sponges (if you have a back wall or internal filter). These physically (mechanically) remove waste from the water column. They basically act like a sieve holding onto all the large particles of waste ready for you to manually remove them from the system.

This tends to be what most people think about when they think of aquarium filters. In reality this is more like the first step of the aquarium filtration process. There are two other forms of filtrations that work alongside mechanical filters that are just as important.

Chemical Filtration

Mechanical filtration may be great for removing those larger particles of waste but they won't remove chemicals and dissolved particles such as coral toxins and metals found within the water column.

The most common type of chemical filtration media used in a saltwater aquarium is activated carbon (charcoal) and Granular Ferric Oxide (GFO). Both these materials remove impurities through tiny chemical/ molecular interactions. Chemical media isn't used as often as biological or mechanical media, but it can be effective for an assortment of filtering purposes.

Many people who use tap water tend to use activated carbon to remove copper and other impurities. Many hobbyists also claim that it can remove any smells from your aquarium and can 'polish' of the water making it look crystal clear. This may not be advertised on the product but there are too many stories of it happening for it to be coincidence.

Whatever media you use for your chemical filtration keep in mind that it will have a certain capacity (a limited amount of chemicals it can remove from the water) and once this capacity has been reached the media will no longer do its job. As a result of this the media needs to be replaced on a regular basis.

For The Beginner – Imagine your chemical filtration media as a sponge and the water from the tap the chemicals you are removing. If the tap was on slow and dripping onto the sponge, the sponge would absorb the water. However in time the sponge would fill up with water and won't be able to hold anymore so the water would start to fall from the sponge. This is exactly what happens with the chemical media in our aquariums and this is why we have to replace our media.

Always follow the guidance on the media instructions as to how long it will last before it needs replacing.

Biological Filtration

In a saltwater aquarium biological filtration is the most important. In theory (and this is in theory as I don't recommend this) you could run your aquarium with no mechanical or chemical filtration, your livestock would not necessarily suffer from losing these two forms of filtration. However if you had no biological filtration, your whole aquarium would suffer.

Biological filtration forms when naturally occurring bacteria establish a colony on and within your aquarium. These bacteria process toxic chemicals, such as Ammonia, and turn them into less toxic chemicals, such as Nitrate.

In order to establish a strong colony of bacteria (for your biological filtration) you will need to let your aquarium go through the nitrogen cycle, the process of growing bacteria.

See Step 7a – The Nitrogen Cycle, for more information on biological filtration. This section explains what the nitrogen cycle is and what it does (In a nut shell bacteria break down waste to nitrate).

There are commonly two groups of bacteria you want to grow within your filter media, Aerobic and Facultative (Not Anaerobic, I will explain why) bacteria.

Aerobic Bacteria

These are the species of bacteria that require oxygen for their basic survival, growth and reproduction. Bacteria that are exposed to high levels of oxygen are the Nitrifiers. These are the bacteria that turn ammonia into nitrate. Almost every aquarium will house this type of bacteria, without them there would be no nitrogen cycle.

Aerobic Bacteria grow on every surface found within your aquarium. Live rock was once primarily used in bulk to house as much bacteria as possible but with advances in the hobby this is no longer the case. A modern alternative is the use of porous filter media such as siporax, maxspect blocks and bio pure balls. These can house all the bacteria an aquarium needs in a small amount of space.

If you place this type of filter media in a high/medium flow area you will have the ideal environment to house and grow aerobic bacteria.

Facultative Bacteria

Nitrate is consumed by facultative bacteria not anaerobic bacteria. Facultative bacteria can switch from the use of Oxygen to NO3 (Nitrate) when the Oxygen supply is low. This switch normally occurs when the oxygen level is less than 0.5 mg/L but the ideal levels are less than 0.5 and greater than 0.1. This is called an anoxic zone.

It is within this zone (low oxygen levels) that denitrification occurs. This is where bacteria consume Nitrate or Nitrite. For example; once all the oxygen has been consumed by the bacteria, in order to stay alive, the bacteria will turn to nitrate for their oxygen supply. With the combination of a carbon source (this is your nitrate remover) the bacteria break down the nitrate, consume the oxygen from the nitrate and release nitrogen gas as a waste product. Thus removing nitrate from your water column.

As facultative bacteria need low levels of oxygen to consume nitrate you are going to want your filter media (where the bacteria will grow) in a lower flow area (where oxygen levels are lower). Filter media blocks are ideal for this as the facultative bacteria will live on the inside of the block and aerobic bacteria will populate the outer area of the block.

The process of removing nitrate is the next stage in the nitrogen cycle. By housing both types of bacteria within the aquarium you can successfully convert ammonia to nitrate and then nitrate to nitrogen gas.

Anaerobic bacteria live in zero Oxygen environments. They convert organics to water, Carbon Dioxide, and Methane (Hydrogen Sulphide is also a product). You do not want your reef to have anaerobic conditions anywhere. The sulphur dead spots that some people refer to are anaerobic. This happens when a filter media or in most cases a deep sand bed become impacted and the diffusion of gas does not take place. The release of sulphur can have a devastating effect on a reef tank and wipe out livestock.

For the Beginner – Understanding how the full nitrogen cycle works within a saltwater aquarium can often seem confusing and overwhelming. Understanding how aerobic and facultative bacteria work can be even worse. My recommendation for the beginner is to use some form of bio block for your biological filter media. Maxspec blocks are one of the ones I use.

They have a huge surface area. Meaning a single block is like a multi-storey hotel for bacteria. The bacteria on the outside of the block have access to oxygen and the bacteria on the inside of the block have limited access to oxygen. One block can therefore house both types of bacteria. This should take care of the nitrogen cycle within your aquarium.

If nitrate is an issue once your aquarium is running then moving the media block to a low flow area will lower how much oxygen rich water gets to the block. This will increase the number of facultative bacteria on that media block. These are the ones that consume nitrate. More bacteria means more nitrate can be consumed.

So, to recap; Food/waste in your aquarium will break down (rot) and produce ammonia. Naturally occurring bacteria will consume ammonia into Nitrite and then to Nitrate. Nitrate is the safest of the three forms of waste. These bacteria need oxygen to survive and do their job. If there is little oxygen the bacteria will use the oxygen found in nitrate and produce nitrogen gas as waste. This gas then bubbles up to the surface of your aquarium and leaves the water. This is a very basic explanation of the full nitrogen cycle.

If you do have any issues with nitrate or the nitrogen cycle then please feel free to email me. Every aquarium is different and my advice on how to fix a problem will most likely be specific to your system. If email is not an option then I would recommend going to your LFS (Local fish store) to ask for advice.

Conclusion

In order to maintain a successful saltwater aquarium all three forms of filtration should ideally be used. As stated earlier you can manage on just biological, but for the best results you should use mechanical and chemical alongside it. They can be used in any form of filtration unit from internal filters to complex sumps, the only difference is what you use for each form of filtration.

For example, if you have a sump your mechanically filtration may be a filter sock and your chemical filtration may be media in a reactor. If you have a back wall filter, your mechanical filtration may be mesh/ sponge pads and your chemical filtration may be activated carbon in a mesh bag in one of your filters chambers.

There are many ways to filter a saltwater aquarium and all are personal to each hobbyists. All have some basic similarities but how you use biological, mechanical and chemical filtration in your own aquarium is up to you.

Now we know what types of filtration there are, let's look at some of the filtration units (that house the Chemical, Mechanical and Biological filtration) many hobbyists use.

Step 2b

Types of Filtration Units

So I'm hoping by now you have a rough idea of what type of aquarium you are wanting, if not go back to step 1. Remember there is no rush; patience in this hobby is a must which is something I failed to learn in the beginning.

So I am guessing you are like me and didn't go back to step 1 and just carried on reading? Correct?

Well not to worry, I'm sure you will revisit step 1 if needed at a later date.

Let's begin step 2...

In order to keep any marine aquarium up and running you are going to need a filtration unit to help clean, circulate and oxygenate your water.

There are generally four main types of filtration units used within the hobby;

Internal Filtration Units

Internal filtration units are housed within the aquarium itself. They are generally cheaper to use and are more commonly used on fish only systems and freshwater aquariums. This type of filtration is rather uncommon among saltwater hobbyist. Internal units are simply not efficient enough to support a marine environment. Not to mention keeping all that equipment in your display is very unsightly.

I personally don't recommend this form of filtration for a saltwater aquarium. All I am doing here is covering the basics and making you aware that it's an option.

The only time internal filters are used within the saltwater hobby are within the quarantine tank for water movement.

External Filtration Units

Another option is an external filtration unit such as a canister filter or hang on filter. Again this is not necessarily a very common form of filtration among hobbyists but they are used.

Many hobbyists have found that canister filters are problematic when it comes to parameter control (such as nitrates) and others have used them on reef aquariums for years. The key to success when using a canister filters is regular maintenance. Those who never have a problem with their filters are the ones who clean them out often.

I personally don't recommend using one as I don't believe they are efficient enough for a saltwater tank. This is simply my opinion (and not fact) as they are widely used and have been successful. There are simply too many stories where canister filters have failed and a tank has crashed for me to put my trust into using them.

It really comes down to what type of aquarium you want to keep;

Fish only system, yes. Reef tank, no.

Again, this is only my opinion based on my own personal experience. If you decided based on your own research and experiences that an external filter is ideal for your system, then go for it!

Built In/ Back Wall Filtration Units

This filtration unit is built into the aquarium itself. They are most commonly built into the back of the aquarium leaving the display with a nice clean and clutter free finish. Most of your equipment will be kept out of sight in this area. The back section itself is normally broken down into chambers (to promote water flow throughout the unit) where you can keep a wide range of equipment and filter media.

Most Nano aquariums have a built in filter and many hobbyists have had great success with this form of filtration (Drew's Lagoon is one for example). I started off with a Nano aquarium that had a back wall filter unit and it worked a treat. It was somewhat easy to clean and I could easily see (though the back of the tank) when detritus and waste started to build up.

The only flaw I, and others, have had with a built in filtration unit is the limited space available within them. You are normally very restricted with space once you have added heaters, filter media, skimmers etc. into the chambers. That equipment you do buy often needs to be designed for a Nano aquarium in order to properly fit into the chambers. It's not a huge issue but it does cause some restrictions with what equipment you can fit into the back wall unit.

The Sump

A sump is a separate tank that is connected to your main display tank via pumps and pipes.

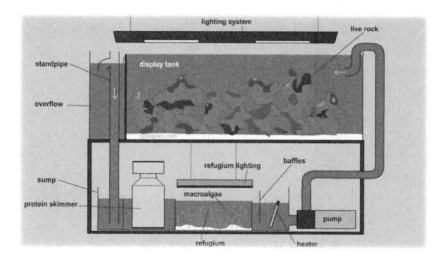

This separate tank is your filtration unit. They are suitable for every kind of marine aquarium and are one of the most widely used forms of filtration units.

Because they are awesome!

There are so many reasons why a sumped tank is ideal, but I'm only going to list the ones that I personally have found that have made my life easier;

1 - A Place for that Equipment

There is nothing more annoying than looking at your beautiful, natural aquarium where your fish are swimming and going about their daily lives and you see a huge black filter or heater spoiling the view.

One of my aquariums had all my equipment within the display area and it looked cluttered. It took up so much space where I wanted corals and it wasn't the look I had in mind when I pictured my reef. It bugged me for weeks until I finally got a sump. FINALLY my aquarium was clear of equipment and had the natural look I was aiming for.

2 – It's Easy

Having a sump makes getting to your equipment for maintenance so much easier. There are no fish or corals in the way; there is no worry that you will injure a fish in the process or about knocking over your rock structure.

It simply makes life easier.

You also have easy access to the water within your aquarium for testing and water changes.

3 - More Water

It increases your water volume which is always a plus. More water normally means less hassle with your parameters and a tank capable of a higher bio load and more fish. In some cases it can double your aquariums water volume.

4 - Filtration

A sump is the ideal place for mechanical (a filter sock), chemical (a reactor full of carbon) and biological (the rock and media) filtration to occur all out of sight under your display tank.

It's your aquarium and your decision. So as with anything in this hobby make sure you do your homework and find out what is best for you. Based on trial and error I have found out a sump proves to be a valuable tool for any hobbyists with any size aquarium. If you have the space and a sump is possible, go for it. If not, then I recommend the use of a back wall filter or external filter unit.

For the Beginner – I recommend you get an aquarium with a built in filter or a sumped aquarium. These are by far the best two options for a beginner.

I would suggest using a filter sock if you have a sump or some filter floss if you have a back wall filter for your mechanical filteration. For your chemical filtration I would simply use carbon in a bag placed in the sump or back wall unit. Finally, for your biological filter media I would use a form of media block. Simply place the media in your filtration unit and you are good to go. For smaller back wall units you can buy media balls. These are the same as the media blocks but are designed to fit into the smaller filtration units.

At this stage in your aquariums life there is no need to over complicate it. Keep it simple and it will work. As you expand within the hobby then you can change and improve your filtration.

As I don't know what aquarium you have, suggesting what filtration you use is challenging. If you have a standard aquarium then the above will work just fine but if you have a unique aquarium and are struggling with what to do then please email me. Together we can talk about what is best for you and your aquariums specific needs.

As I explained before the main thing I use my filter for is a place to store all that equipment. So let's take a look at what some of that equipment might be...

Step 3

Equipment

One of the biggest questions people face when setting up their aquarium is, **what equipment do I need**?

Most know you need to control the temperature with a chiller or heater but what else? What is a 'Protein Skimmer' or a 'reactor'? And what the hell is a refugium?

Questions on the topic of equipment are probably the most commonly asked. Our whole underwater ecosystems are kept alive and stable by equipment, knowing what equipment to get and why you will need it is a must.

Personally, my biggest issue was not what equipment I needed (as most sites and books state what equipment you will need) it was not knowing what that equipment did, why/if I needed it and how I set it up in my aquarium. Hopefully within this step I can clarify this for you!

Within this section you can find a list of the equipment that many hobbyists use. Some are deemed essential and others are helpful extras.

For the Beginner – This list will include a wide range of equipment. As a beginner some of this equipment you will need and others you can simply add later if needed. After each section I will give my recommendations on if you need this piece of equipment to begin with. As this is simply my advice and option you don't have to follow it if you want to do it differently! Remember, it's your aquarium.

Protein Skimmer

When I started off I had no idea what a Protein Skimmer was. I came from a freshwater aquarium background so I knew the basic need for filtration but I never heard of a skimmer.

The 'not knowing' was a huge setback for me. I didn't know what one was so I avoided getting one. It's the reasons it took me so long to get into the hobby. The whole not knowing really set me back years.

Later in the hobby I ended up getting a small Nano skimmer that was relatively cheap, just to see what they did and if it would benefit my system.

Safe to say the cheap one was rubbish. It was so much more hassle than it was worth. In a fit of rage I binned it and ordered a more expensive one. Obviously I sulked like a baby until the new one turned up...

...but getting the better skimmer was the best thing I did.

What it is? What it Does?

A Protein Skimmer is a piece of equipment that is used within the marine aquarium to remove waste from the water column. Although they are not essential they are a great addition to any saltwater aquarium.

There are many types of Protein Skimmers that come in a range of shapes and sizes but they all do the same job in virtually the same way.

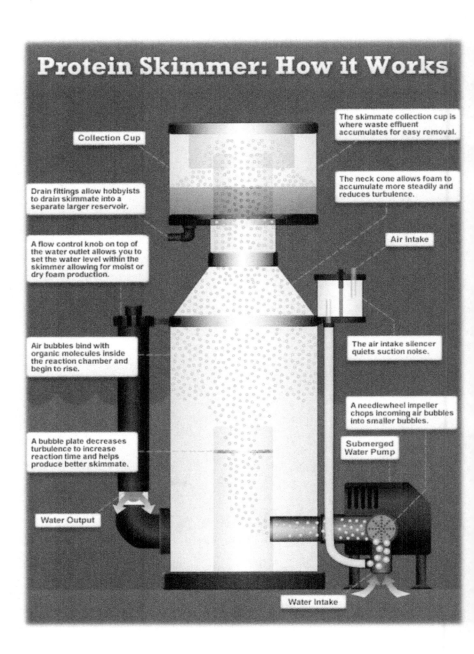

Protein Skimmer: How it Works

Collection Cup

The skimmate collection cup is where waste effluent accumulates for easy removal.

Drain fittings allow hobbyists to drain skimmate into a separate larger reservoir.

The neck cone allows foam to accumulate more steadily and reduces turbulence.

A flow control knob on top of the water outlet allows you to set the water level within the skimmer allowing for moist or dry foam production.

Air Intake

Air bubbles bind with organic molecules inside the reaction chamber and begin to rise.

The air intake silencer quiets suction noise.

A needlewheel impeller chops incoming air bubbles into smaller bubbles.

A bubble plate decreases turbulence to increase reaction time and helps produce better skimmate.

Submerged Water Pump

Water Output

Water Intake

A Protein Skimmer (also referred to as a foam fractionator) is a piece of equipment used in a saltwater aquarium in order to remove dissolved organic compounds and other harmful substances that need to be removed from the aquarium water column. If these organics are not removed they can breakdown in the aquarium (or filter) and add to the biological load.

They remove these dissolved organic compounds (let's use DOC for short as typing this over and over will get a tad repetitive) from the water using air bubbles that are collected in a collection cup. As the air and water are mixed in the skimmers chamber the bubbles rise and take with them the DOC that are attracted to the bubbles surface. When the bubbles with the proteins, DOC and other nasty stuff bubble up the skimmer they are collected in the skimmers collection cup where they can be removed from the aquarium.

Think about the ocean, when the waves crash on the shore you sometimes see a lot of foam nearby. This is the ocean water mixing with the air as the waves hit the land. The foam is waste that has been removed from the water and often ends up been washed up the beach. This is one way nature removes waste from the ocean. As we don't have waves, crashing or shores in our aquariums we will have to settle with the Protein skimmer.

For the Beginner – If the above is confusing then this is a very basic explanation of what one is. A protein skimmer mixes air bubbles with water. Waste in your aquariums water 'sticks' to the bubbles as they rise in the skimmers body. These 'dirty' bubbles then collect in the cup at the top. Over the course of a few days this cup will fill up with gunk and thick dirty water. This 'gunk' is the broken down fish poo, detritus and uneaten food.

This process means the waste is removed from the water before it breaks down into ammonia, phosphate, nitrate etc. helping to keep your aquarium parameters as stable as possible. This is ultimately what a skimmer does. They remove waste from the water.

Why it's Useful?

Some advantages of getting a Protein Skimmer are;

- Skimmers can act like the lungs of the aquarium. As they mix water with air they help increase the dissolved oxygen levels in an aquarium.

- As stated above they remove DOC before they get a chance to breakdown. Fewer DOC's means less will breakdown which means less nitrate and phosphate in your aquarium.

- They can help lead to a more stable pH since less DOC are in the system and more aeration is occurring. Oxygen and carbon dioxide levels in your water have a direct impact on the pH level. The air flow in the skimmer helps to keep oxygen and carbon dioxide levels stable resulting in a more stable pH.

There are a few drawbacks to a protein skimmer such as noise and cost, but I personally would not go without having one in a fully stocked, mature system. The noise isn't really a problem to most as once a skimmer is in your cabinet you can't really hear it.

Which one to get?

TIP – *Don't buy a cheap skimmer, it's worth saving up and getting a recommended make such as a tunze, nyos or bubble mag.*

There are two main types of protein skimmer, Air Stone and Pump skimmers.

Air Stone

This is a simple skimmer design that uses an air stone to produce the bubbles. These days they are less common than the pump kind but still effective. These tend to be cheaper than other skimmers but you normally have to buy the air stone and skimmer body separately.

Pump Skimmers

They use a pump to supply the water movement and drag the air from the surface mechanically. Pump skimmers are more commonly found within the home aquarium as they are readily available. I personally prefer these skimmers to the air stone ones. Advances in technology over the years have resulted in some easy to use, yet still very effective, skimmers.

For The Beginner - Skimmers will have a recommended aquarium size on their instructions so finding one that fits your size system is easy.

Setting Up The Skimmer

Most beginners struggle to get their protein skimmer set so it produces a good skim. Changing the settings on most skimmers can be done in one of two ways.

Tip - This section will make a lot more sense when you physically have your skimmer and you can see what I mean. So if for now it doesn't make too much sense, then don't worry too much as this is expected.

One

You can change the depth you have your skimmer in your water. Most companies have a recommended water level for each of their skimmers, unfortunately this does not always work for everybody. If your skimmer is acting up and overflowing then you should raise the skimmer a little bit. This can be done by simply placing something under the skimmer (something that will be safe in the water). Getting the correct water level may take a while so you may have to change the height a few times.

Two

Controlling how much water flows through the skimmer. Most skimmers allow you to control the outlet of the water, opening and closing the valve to change the water level in the skimmer. As you play around with the valve you will see the water level going up and down. Setting the skimmer takes time and this can be rather frustrating. Each skimmer has its recommended water level inside the skimmer so I suggest you start of from there and change as you need to.

When changing the skimmers water level you will need to leave it for a day or two between changes as it takes time for the change to take effect. Small changes are better than large ones so always go slow and steady and monitor your results.

For the Beginner – For a newly set up aquarium with low livestock levels you could go without one. Your waste levels with low stock will be manageable through good filtration and regular water changes.

If you go with a small aquarium (like the fluval evo) you can live without a skimmer full stop. It will mean more water changes and more manual cleaning but your aquarium won't suffer from not having one.

If you go with a bigger aquarium then I recommend getting a skimmer. Bigger aquariums mean more livestock which means more waste to manage. In a bigger aquarium doing a large water change isn't as easy either. So the extra filtration comes in handy.

My personal rule of thumb is if you have a sump filter then get a skimmer. If you have a back wall filter and are tight on space then go without. As most large aquariums come with sump filters and many Nano aquariums come with back wall filters this supports the above statement.

In terms of setting up the skimmer for the first time I would follow the instructions and leave it for a few days to settle in before you make any other changes. Then leave or change accordingly to the skim you get from it.

Lighting

By now I am hoping you have a good idea of what type of livestock you want to keep within your aquarium.

Well I hope so as this ultimately decides what type of lighting you will need.

If all you are wanting are fish then your lighting choice is relatively easy as almost any aquarium light well be fine to use. The difficulty comes when you want to keep livestock that requires a good light source to survive, such as photosynthetic creatures. Your everyday aquarium light will simply not do...

On the bright side (light pun, sorry) there are lights out there that have been designed with these creatures in mind. But which one do you chose...

Well before we get into what type of lighting you should use, let's talk a little about Light itself.

This section is for no other reason than it's useful to know, especially if you want to keep creatures that depend on light for their survival.

PUR and PAR

Two measurements that are often used when talking about light are PUR and PAR.

PAR – Photosynthetically Active Radiation

PAR is the number of light particles that fall within a square meter over the course of one second. It essentially measures the brightness of light. Corals need a certain level of PAR in order to photosynthesize, not too much and not too little. Too much or too little PAR can harm the coral and prevent it from producing food.

Basically, think of PAR as the brightness of light in the visual spectrum (the light we can see with our eyes).

PUR – Photosynthetically Useable Radiation

PUR is basically the usable portion of PAR.

For example;

If we have a reading of 400 PAR, that 400 is made up from a variety of light from the spectrum (blue, green, red etc.).

The photosynthetic needs differ from coral to coral. Although many may prefer the same level of PAR, Some will prefer blue light and some will prefer a red light.

A bright blue light and a bright red light may have the same brightness (PAR) but they have a different spectrum/ colour (PUR).

Basically PUR is what colour (wavelength) the Light (PAR) is made up form.

The reason for this is that different wavelengths of light (Colours) are filtered in water at different depths. Blue light penetrates deeper in water than red light does. So corals that are naturally found deeper in water will have evolved to use more blue light than red in their process of photosynthesis.

So even if we get the brightness of light correct if it's made up of mainly red light, our corals (who prefer blue light) won't be too happy. This would be a case of having the correct PAR but the incorrect PUR. So giving corals a good amount of PAR is great, but that PAR needs to be at the right PUR for it to be useful and beneficial for corals.

Confused? Don't worry. Understanding the complexity of light isn't going to happen overnight (another light pun, sorry again). All I wanted to do here was to give you a brief understanding of PUR and PAR as these two measurements are used often within the hobby.

Some experienced reefers measure the levels of PAR and PUR within their systems to ensure they pick the best place to mount a coral. I personally have never tested my tanks PAR and PUR as I only keep soft corals these days. I normally adjust my light intensity gradually to see what my corals prefer. If your corals are sulking chances are your lights need adjusting. If you are going to keep more sensitive corals then getting the ideal PAR and PUR levels in your aquarium is essential for their wellbeing and general health.

For The Beginner – to recap; PUR is the intensity of the light and PAR is the colour of the light. Photosynthetic creatures need a certain colour and intensity to survive.

So...

Let's go back to talking about the types of lighting you can use for your aquarium.

There are two main types of lights used within the hobby, T5 florescent tube lighting and LED.

T5 Florescent Tube

T5 is simply a collective term for a narrow-diameter fluorescent light tube.

T5's are reasonably priced (much cheaper than LED units) and are becoming more popular within the hobby. They are easy to set up and the fact they work straight out of the box is a real bonus for many hobbyists! You simply plug them in and you are good to go. They have been designed with corals in mind and are already set to the necessary PAR and PUR needed for keeping most photosynthetic creatures.

There are however two minor drawbacks with the T5's.

The first is that they tend to give off a lot of heat when in use.

For most this is not an issue but it has been known for this excess heat to have an effect on the aquariums overall temperature. I imagine this is only an issue for Nano aquariums (with a small water volume) in a small room. A room with adequate ventilation should eliminate this issue but I feel it's worth a mention.

The second is although the unit is cheap to buy; you will have to replace the tube on a regular basis. With typical usage of 8-12 hours per day each bulb should be replaced after a period of 9-12 months.

T5 tubes are very popular within the hobby as they are efficient and easy to use. If you do struggle when setting up your lights your Local Fish Store will most likely be able to offer you some guidance or you can email me directly and we can work through your particular issue.

If you are on a budget, the t5's might be a good option to look into as their initial set up cost is low.

LED

LED (Light Emitting Diode) lights are fast becoming the most popular choice of lighting within the hobby for many reasons.

LED's consume a lot less power than the T5's and they tend to give off less heat. Many units come with a full spectrum range of light that are adjustable to suit every need. You can customise your lighting to produce any level of PAR and PUR that you desire.

LED's are unfortunately a lot more expensive than t5's which is off putting for many hobbyists. The only thing I will say is LED's don't need replacing as often as the T5's, making the LED cheaper in the long run.

Personally I (and many other hobbyists) prefer LED's and as time goes on they are only getting better. The fact LED's are fully customizable in terms of PAR and PUR is a huge win as they can sustain any photosynthetic creature in any style of aquarium.

There are many makes and models of LED units that all work well. It really all comes down to how much money you are wanting to spend as some light units can cost as much as the tank itself, if not more. If you are serious about keeping high end corals then it's well worth paying that little bit extra for the high quality units.

Many hobbyists use a combination of T5 and LED lighting to ensure they are giving the corals exactly what they need. This is however optional as both the t5 and LED light units will work well on their own.

As with everything in this hobby, it all comes down to personal preference. I have seen reef tanks grow and do great on both types of lighting. There is no 'best one' for corals. Both work very well alone or as a combination!

For the Beginner – Understanding light isn't something a beginner needs to know in detail and until I wrote this book I didn't really understand it fully myself. All you need to know is that photosynthetic creates need light to survive. Not too much and not too little. If you use T5 lighting then you simply plug and pay. If you use LED lighting then you need to spend some time to adjust the intensity of your lights to suit the livestock within your aquarium. We will go into detail later in this book about setting up your lights to suit your livestock. For now you just need to decide if you will go with T5 or LED.

If you have an all in one aquarium most come with a built in light unit so you don't have to worry about choosing one. If your aquarium doesn't come with a light, then I personally suggest LED lighting for their customisable option to suit every style of aquarium. Most LED units have some instructions as to their ideal settings so I would start with that before you make some adjustments yourself.

Heater/Chiller

Those coming from a 'tropical freshwater aquarium' background will know all too well that if you wish to keep these beautiful creatures then you need to keep the water at a correct and constant temperature.

Those who are just entering the aquarium hobby, you need to know if you want to keep these beautiful creatures then you need to keep the water at a correct and constant temperature...

The recommended temperature for a reef tank is 26.C (Degrees Celsius), but an acceptable range of 24-27 is what most hobbyists consider reef safe.

This is normally achieved in one of two ways...

A Heater

or

A chiller

For obvious reasons you use a heater if the temperature where you will keep the tank is cooler than 26C and you use a chiller if the temperature is above 26C. As I am located in England, I use a heater. My only issue occurs during the summer months when I need to keep an eye on my reef as the house temperature tends to rise above 26C. This is nothing a simple frozen bottle of water sitting in my sump can't fix but seasonal temperature changes might be something you need to think about.

I don't think I need to go into detail of what a heater is and does and the same goes for a chiller. Both can be set to achieve a specific temperature and there are many brands of both.

The only thing I would recommend is to get a second thermostat to record the temperature of your aquarium. This is more of a failsafe to ensure the thermostat on the heater/chiller is accurate.

All you need to do is get the equipment that is suitable for your size aquarium (heater or chiller depending on what you need) and you are good to go.

Remember, consistency is key!

You don't want to make any sudden changes. If you need to make any temperature changes then you need to do so gradually and over the course of a few days.

TIP – Whatever you need to control your temperature (be it a chiller or heater) it's worthwhile getting a separate thermometer. This is simply a failsafe to ensure the heater/chiller doesn't malfunction. If both the heater/chiller and the thermometer are reading the same temperature, everything is ok. If they are reading a different temperature to each other, then you know there is a problem with one of them.

I know I have mentioned this above but I have seen aquariums crash as the water temperature was way out. A cheap and simple thermometer could prevent this.

Wave-maker

Almost everyone who owns a fish tank knows that you need a light, some form of filtration and a heater/chiller. These are some of the most commonly used pieces of equipment needed in an aquarium and most beginners already know they need these three.

But what most people don't know is adequate water flow within a marine aquarium is crucial for a healthy reef. Good flow around the display tank is essential for coral health, the oxidisation of water and it prevents waste from building up on the rock or floor of the tank.

This is where a wave maker comes in handy...

When I say good flow, I don't mean flow so strong that the water in your aquarium splashes around and your fish look like they are in a thunder storm. Have you seen Finding Nemo? He didn't do so well when he was in the bag been shaken up by the little girl. That was way too much water movement!

You need just the right level of flow.

Basically, all we are trying to do is mimic the ocean waves and water movement. Everything we do revolves around trying to mimic our livestock's natural environment as much as possible and a wave maker is an essential piece of equipment that allows us to do just that.

So before we get into details about what a wave maker is, let's talk about water flow;

Basics of Flow

One of the most under-rated aspects in a saltwater aquarium is flow. Water movement is essential to maintaining a healthy aquarium.

One benefit of good flow is it prevents detritus from building up. With enough flow, detritus isn't allowed to settle on the substrate of your aquarium. If it's allowed to settle it will begin to rot and decompose, resulting in an increase in nitrates.

By keeping the detritus in the water column it will be picked up by your mechanical filtration units, such as filter socks or filter mats. Regular cleaning of the socks/mats will remove the waste from the water column.

In fish only with live rock (FOWLR) and reef systems having ample flow becomes even more important as live rock is often the main filtration in these type of aquariums. Meaning good flow is essential to sustain a health colony of beneficial bacteria. An even higher flow rate than what is needed to keep detritus moving is recommended when using live rock as filtration. This isn't as common these days as most use media designed for filtration but it is worth noting.

How Much Flow is Needed?

Flow within an aquarium is measured in total tank turnovers per hour. This is the amount of times the total aquariums water volume is pumped through your pumps/wave makers per hour.

There is a basic equation for this;

Total flow of the pumps/wave maker ÷ Total tank volume

For example;

If a 20 gallon tank had one power head pushing 100 gph (gallons per hour), then the equation would be;

$$100 \div 20 = 5$$

So the overall tank turn over per hour is 5.

FO tank flow – FO (Fish Only) tanks generally need the lowest flow. From 15x turnover to 20x turnover should be enough flow to keep detritus from settling on the substrate.

FOWLR flow – FOWLR (Fish Only with Live Rock) systems will need more flow to get water to the filtering bacteria. 20x turnover is a recommended minimum.

Reef flow – Reef tank flow will start out at the same FOWLR guideline of 20x turnover, but depending on coral type this could be all the way up to 100x turnover or more...

Low flow (20x-30x) – Several types of corals do very well in low flow conditions such as: zoanthids, palythoas, some leathers, most large polyp stony (LPS) and many others.

Medium flow (30x-40x) – Most of the corals from the low flow group will also do well in medium flow. Medium flow also adds a few very fast growers such as xenia and more species of leather coral.

High flow (40x-100x) – Some of the low and medium flow corals will do ok if placed out of direct flow up past the 50x turnover mark. Corals from the medium flow group such as: xenia and leathers will still thrive in high flow. Fleshy LPS will have to be placed in a relatively dead spot to survive in a high flow aquarium. 50x + turnover introduces a whole new group of corals known as small polyp stony (SPS). SPS coral need very high flow to keep its polyps clear of waste.

What are the Types of Flow Found within an Aquarium?

When I say types of flow I mean how the water is moving around your display tank.

Think back to when you were a kid in the bath, you would make waves moving back and forward, well this is one type of flow.

Now picture a washing machine, the water spins around the drum, this is another type of flow.

FO and FOWLR tanks will do well with most types of flow as long as there is enough. Reef systems however demand more chaotic flow to keep coral healthy and growing.

Laminar Flow – Laminar flow is unidirectional. You will usually end up with this type of flow when you have only one source of flow.

Alternating Flow – Alternating flow is most comparable to a wave motion. The water pushes forward then back in a rhythmic motion. This is the type of flow you will get from a wave maker or on particular settings.

Random Chaotic – Random Chaotic flow is usually the best choice. It is easily achieved with the use of several wave makers pointed to converge in the tank.

...And what produces flow in an aquarium? A Wave maker.

For The Beginner - All I would say is just make sure you have enough water movement. If it looks to calm then it probably is.

Flow is simply the movement of water. Image the air in your car. With all the windows closed there is little air movement (no wave makers and little flow). If you roll down one window there is a lot of air movement in one area and it comes from one direction (one wave maker and laminar flow). If you roll down all the windows your hair is going to go all over and there will be a lot of wind. (many wave makers and random chaotic flow).

All the above types of flow are achievable within any aquarium though the use of wave makers. Many of these wave makers have settings that vary from model to model so don't worry if you do not really understand the types of flow. The wave maker will have each type saved as a setting for you to choose from.

So a Wave maker...

What it is?

Wavemakers are literally, wave makers.

They are water surge devices that produce waves within the aquarium. The overall goal of this is to try to re-create the same conditions found within the oceans.

What is Does?

They basically produce flow within the aquarium.

Yes, that's it, but it's an essential aspect of any saltwater aquarium.

Once you have an understanding of what flow is and why it's important in an aquarium all you need to really know are the two key points below;

One - That each wave maker is different and produces different types of water movement depending on what setting you have them on.

Some wave makers have settings that allow you to change the type of flow in the tank (the types of flow explained before).

Each hobbyist is different and has a prefer type of flow they desire in their aquarium.

Two - Remember the Goldilocks rule - you need just the right amount of flow, not too little and not too much.

The combination of 1 and 2 is all you need.

TIP – if your corals have no movement then you might want more flow. If they look like they are getting blown about you might want to dial your wave maker down a setting or two. You can often tell just by looking what flow is best based on coral and fish movement.

If you have a small aquarium a small wave maker will do, if you have a large aquarium you will need a few wave makers to produce enough flow. You can use many small ones in a large aquarium or a few large ones; it's totally up to you as every aquarium is different.

Something as simple as the layout of the rock in the aquarium can determine how many wave makers you will need and where you will need to place them. Like I said, each tank is different.

There are many advantages to having a wave maker in your aquarium. They far out weight the disadvantages of having one as the only negative aspect I can think of is the little noise they make and the little space they take up in the aquarium.

Many of the advantages are;

Helps keep the fish healthy
In their natural habitat fish and inverts are exposed to constant water movement as the ocean waves don't sleep. To mimic the fish's natural habitat a wave maker is essential.

Prevents dead spots
A dead spot is a place in the tank where there is low/no water flow. As a result of this waste, detritus and left over food gets left in this section of the tank. Over time this builds up and rots resulting in poor water quality. No dead spots = no waste build up = better water quality. It's that simple.

Keeps coral and inverts healthy
Many corals and inverts don't move around the aquarium. They need the water flow to bring food, nutrients and oxygen to within their reach. If you want to keep these types of stationary creatures healthy then good flow is essential.

They add to the overall visual appeal of the tank
Flow causes corals to sway like grass in the wind, it stimulates fish to become more active and gives the aquarium an overall natural look.

Overall it's fair to say that no reef tank is complete without a wave maker and they are now a must have in terms of essential equipment.

For the Beginner – For a beginner just starting off you may get away with not having a wave maker. In a small aquarium (50 litres or less) you might have enough flow with just your return pump.

If you do have a larger aquarium then getting a wave maker for that extra bit of flow will be a good idea. Both your fish and corals will benefit from doing this.

I would recommend starting off with one wave maker and place it opposite to your return pumps nozzle. This will produce the best flow to begin with. From here simply keep an eye on your flow. Your rock scape has a huge impact on your overall flow so you may need to move the wave maker if flow in parts of the aquarium are very low. What I would do is place the wave maker opposite your return pump and leave it there for a few days. If you start to see a build-up of detritus in certain areas then move the wave maker so it stirs up this detritus. Leave it for a few days and see what happens.

If you are still finding areas of detritus then it may be a good idea to either rearrange your rock scape (to help with flow) or get a second wave maker.

Commonly Asked Questions – Wave Maker Placement?

This is a hard question to answer without seeing your set up. The size of your tank, the shape of your tank, the rock layout and coral placements are all factors that determine where you should place your wave maker. You want to eliminate as many dead spots as possible and ensure there is enough movement on the surface of the water while making sure the corals get the flow they need.

TIP – *It's a case of working with your return pump and planning out the best fit for your system. The most common placement that I have seen in home aquariums is on the side wall of the tank opposite the return pumps outlet. I recommend starting out in this position first and moving your wave maker around if needed.*

It's so difficult to give advice on wave makers. Each tank setup has a unique flow pattern so there is no one correct method.

The only thing that goes for all marine aquariums is that a wave maker is an essential piece of equipment and flow is a must!

Media Reactor
(Optional – for the most part)

A media reactor is an advanced method used for chemical filtration in saltwater aquariums. These devices look very different from traditional aquarium filters. They have a tube-like design with an input and output valve located at the top of the device.

The tube itself can be filled with the filter media of your choice. These devices typically utilize the up-flow principle in order to fluidize chemical filtration media thereby increasing its efficacy. The water is evenly distributed throughout the reactor increasing surface area contact with the filter media. These units are available in multiple sizes ranging from a mini size for Nano aquariums to bigger devices for larger aquariums.

Types of Filter Media

There are several choices of media depending on the type of reactor you choose. One of the most popular types of reactor is the PhosBan reactor. This device helps to absorb and remove phosphates and other pollutants from the aquarium. High phosphate levels in the aquarium have been linked to a number of problems including algae growth. Installing one of these devices in your tank has been identified as one of the most effective prevention methods for problem algae. This type of reactor gets its name from the PhosBan filter media which is designed to bind to large amounts of phosphate, removing it from the tanks water column.

Some other types of popular filter media for aquarium reactors include bio pellets, GFO and carbon.

Bio Pellets are exactly what they sound like. They are tiny pellets that can be used as a filter media in a reactor. These pellets are designed to improve water quality by enhancing the nitrification process, removing nitrate and phosphate from the tank water.

GFO stands for granular ferric oxide and is a filter media that is used to remove phosphates and silicates from all types of aquariums. This type of filter media has the largest absorption rates for phosphates and it doesn't tend to leech back into the water like some other filter media (carbon). Some other notable benefits of GFO media is that it won't alter the pH in your tank, it has a high binding capacity and it doesn't take up to much room in the media reactor.

The third type of popular filter media is carbon or, more specifically, activated carbon. Activated carbon is one of the most commonly used types of filter media in a variety of aquarium filters. It is designed specifically for the purification of aquarium water, filtering out toxins and other dissolved wastes in the aquarium water. Carbon comes in a variety of sizes and porosity levels and it generally has a high absorption capacity.

Many hobbyists have never used a reactor and have kept a fully stocked, successful reef tank. It's not a necessity and if you don't run one you won't necessarily fail. I have only recently used one in my aquarium and as stated earlier, they are a great addition to any filtration.

For the Beginner – I personally don't think a beginner just starting out in the hobby needs a media reactor. They are more for the fully stocked, mature systems that are full of corals and need that extra bit of filtration.

All I would do is place the media you want to use (such as carbon) in a media bag and place it in your filter. That is all I do and it works just fine for a basic coral reef tank.

Refractometer

One of the biggest worries many people have when entering the saltwater aquarium hobby is the salty aspect. It's one of our most commonly asked questions from people who are interested in the hobby.

Everyone seems to worry about the salt and how to mix the water to the correct salt level.

Trust me when I say mixing salt is actually rather easy (something I will cover later in this guide). The Key aspect of using salt is to get the correct salt level in your aquarium, ideally one that is stable and matches the oceans salt level.

The salinity level (Specific Gravity Level) in the open ocean is around 1.025 and the average reefer aims to keep their salinity level around 1.024 – 1.026.

Q – What is Specific Gravity?

A – Specific Gravity is the density of an object in relation to a reference liquid. In this case our reference liquid is water (H_2O). Water with no salt in it will give a reading of 1. As we add salt to the water the reading will increase. As hobbyists we want to aim for a reading of 1.024 – 1.026.

Basically all you really need to know is – it's how we find how much salt is in our water and we want to aim for a reading of 1.024 – 1.026.

Within this section I will not cover all the science behind how we read and test how much salt is in the water. To be honest the average hobbyist doesn't need to know this in order to be successful. If you do wish to know more about the science then by all means get in touch via our social media links or email and we can discuss this in detail!

The average hobbyist does however need to know that keeping their salinity level stable and constant is a must!

Just like every other water parameter!

Therefore we need to know what our salt level is. We do this by using refractometer!

Serious hobbyists know that the best way to measure the salinity and specific gravity of aquarium water is to use a refractometer. These precision optical instruments are incredibly accurate even at very low salt levels, and are equally easy to use. Recently, these instruments have become more affordable and I personally believe every hobbyist should have one.

TIP – Try to stay away from other salt measuring tools such as Hydrometers. They are unreliable and inaccurate. I had two of the same make that both had different readings for the same water sample. It is well worth spending that little bit extra and getting an accurate refractometer.

They are so easy to use!

First of all you need to calibrate the refactor to read fresh water at a reading of 1. This is the essential aspect of getting a correct salinity reading. Simply follow the instructions of the make and model of your refractometer to calibrate it for freshwater. Once this is done and your refractometer has been calibrated;

Place 1 to 2 drops of aquarium water onto the prism glass and close the plate cover. Once a fluid sample is placed on the measuring surface, the light passing through it slows and bends. The refractometer focuses this bent light on a tiny internal scale. The scale is magnified by the eyepiece lenses so it is easily visible.

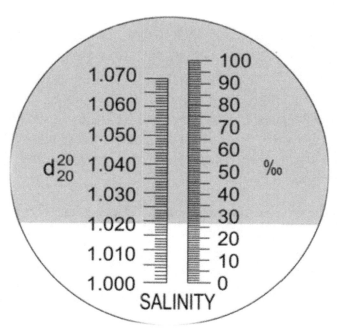

(I shall note that the reading looks low on this, you want to aim for 1.025-26, and the above image is simply an example of what you will see)

Look through the eyepiece and view the scale. The top portion of the scale appears blue and the bottom part appears white. Take your reading at the intersection of these two colours. One side of the scale measures salinity and the other side measures specific gravity.

And that is it!

A refractometer is an essential aspect of every reef and a must have if you are serious about getting into this hobby. They are inexpensive and highly reliable.

I bet if you take a look into any experienced hobbyists cupboards you will find a refractometer and not a hydrometer!

For The Beginner – Refractometers are easy to use and produce accurate results. It's certainly something I recommend every beginner gets. Just remember to calibrate you refractometer with freshwater first.

If you do struggle using one, then by all means get in touch and I can talk you through it or alternatively simply go to your Local Fish Store (LFS) and they will most likely be able to show you exactly how to use the make and model you have.

Refugium

(Optional)

A refugium (a section of a sump tank/external tank designed to keep algae) is one of my favourite sections of a filter.

What is a Refugium?

The photo above is of a basic refugium (not mine, a simple Google image) just to give you an idea of what one is. The basic refugium consists of algae, live rock and substrate (also known as mud) in a separate section to the display tank. The most common place for a refugium is probably the sump.

There are two main functions of a refugium.

The first and by far most important reason is the exportation of nutrients such as nitrates and phosphates. As the algae grows, it uses up nutrients from your aquarium and you simply remove portions of the algae as it grows. Every handful of algae you remove is a handful of nutrients from your tank.

The second reason is to create a natural habitat for pods (tiny creatures) to grown in. It's a safe haven for them to breed and reproduce. Once the pod population grows they get sucked up by the return pump and into the display tank where they become a natural food source for your tanks inhabitants. Pods are macro fauna (small creatures) that live and grow in your aquarium if given the chance. Fish, coral and other livestock feed on these tiny creatures so having them in your aquarium is a good thing.

Refugium Set Up

Substrate
Many people don't use substrate within their refugium as it can gather detritus and be difficult to clean. I personally use miracle mud (a brand of substrate you use in a refugium) as it's great for beneficial bacteria and allows the aquariums copepod population a place to settle. Substrate isn't needed in a successful refugium. It's the same for live rock, many people

have it in their refugium but it is not essential.

Algae
There are many different types of algae used within a refugium. But the easiest, fastest in growth and most commonly used is chaeto macroalgae. You want simple, fast growing algae that are going use up nutrients at a rapid rate. The faster algae will grow the more nutrients it will need to grow, the faster nutrients are removed from the aquariums water and turned into algae.

Lighting
Often this part of the refugium isn't given much thought but this is a critical aspect of algae growth. If you want your corals to grow at a fast rate you supply them with the best lighting possible with the correct PUR and PAR? Or if you want garden plants to grow you make sure they have enough sunlight?

It's the same for cheato growth.

A good quality light is needed to ensure the algae grows at a rapid rate. As algae are plants I would simply use a plant grow light. This tends to have a pink light colouration as this is the ideal PAR for plant photosynthesis.

Mangroves
Totally not necessary but I love them so had to mention it.

These are slow growing trees that have little impact on

removing nutrients in the early stages but they make a great addition to a refugium. It's simply a nice addition to a reef tank and if wanted these can be placed into the main display tank as they are visually appealing.

So there we have it, a basic walk through to a refugium, one of the filtration aspects of my tank that I would not go without. It's natural, low maintenance and highly effective when you use the right lighting.

For The Beginner – A refugium is a very useful, natural method of nutrient removal however it's not essential. For a newly set up aquarium you don't need a refugium. You simply won't have the stock level to produce the needed nutrients to sustain one.

If your nitrates and phosphates start to become a problem then it might be time to invest in a refugium. All I would do at this stage is to keep it simple.

If you do want one then a good quality light and some chaeto macroalgae is all you need. This can be placed anywhere in your filter where there is flow and the algae will get enough light. Many hobbyists who struggle with space in their filter tend to place more 'display friendly' algae in the main aquarium.

As long as there is plenty of light for your algae it doesn't really matter where it's placed in your system. The algae will grow and use up the excess nutrients in your water solving all your problems. All you then have to do is remove some of the algae as it grows to maintain the size you want.

Return Pump

This section only really applies to those that have a sump as you don't use a separate return pump on internal filters and most external, compact filters come with a built in one.

This will also be a relatively short section.

The explanation of what it is and what it does are relatively simple.

A return pump is a large pump that pushes the water from the filter back into the main display tank. As the pump is pushing water against gravity (normally in an upward direction) the pump needs to be relatively powerful.

Most all in one aquariums come fully plumbed with a return pump suitable for the tank size. So for most beginners the need to know about which one is best and what size you should get is non-essential.

However if you are creating your own custom aquarium or need a larger pump because you are running reactors, refugiums etc. from this pump (we will discuss this later) then you might need to know a little about return pumps.

This is also easy to explain as most pumps come with the recommended tank size and flow rate on the packaging. All you need to decide on is; what make and model you want to get and how much flow you will need within your aquarium.

What model you wish to get normally comes down to how

much money you want to spend as each make tends to differ in price. I personally like Jacod and Ecotech pumps, they are silent, have multiple settings and are reliable.

Like I said, this will be a short explanation of what one is.

The only aspect that I will go into detail is on...

Running Other Equipment from Your Pump!

This is a great way of minimising how many pumps you use and it reduces the number of plug sockets that you will need to use (the main reason why I do this).

This is a very simple and effective method of running several pieces of equipment from one pump. All it takes is a little bit of plumbing. You simply T' off some water from your main pipe (the return pipe to the display) and use a ball valve on each pipe to control the flow to each piece of equipment.

The photo below should give you a better idea of what I am talking about...

This method gives you full control over how much flow gets to each piece of equipment.

The only thing you need to consider is the power of the pump, basically you will need a bigger and stronger pump if you intend on running more equipment from it. How big and how strong depends on how many pieces of equipment you want to run.

Personally I use a much larger pump than I need to and run it at around 30% power. This way if you want to add more equipment (like an algae reactor or refugium) then all I need to do is up the power of the pump.

I know this is short, but it is a relatively simple (but highly important) piece of equipment. The one rule to follow is that you get a pump strong enough to produce enough flow in your aquarium and (if you are running equipment from the pump) to your equipment.

For The Beginner – Most all in one aquariums come with their own return pump and plumbing parts so for most beginners this is not something you need to worry about. For your first aquarium I fully recommend you get an aquarium that comes with a back wall filter or a sump filter unit. Doing a custom build for your first aquarium is not recommended.

To start off with I would only have your return pump connected to your display tank. At this stage in your aquariums life that is all you will need. Only advanced hobbyists with a mature system tend to add equipment to the return pumps plumbing.

Filter Sock

(Sump Only)

This is a simple and basic part of most marine aquariums that have a sump. Many hobbyists will never run a system without one and some will never use them. Like many things in this hobby, it's your aquarium and it's your choice.

I would personally use them as I believe they are beneficial. So if you are interested in using a sump and don't fully understand the role of a filter sock then I guess this section is for you!

Many people who are about to read this will think this whole section is pointless...

"A filter sock is such a simple part of an aquarium so why do you need a whole section on it? It's obvious what it is and does?"

Well yes it's a simple piece of equipment but everyone needs to be shown how it works initially. A lack of maintenance on a filter sock can have huge effects on your parameters. A toothbrush and spoon are simple pieces of equipment but someone had to initially show you how to use them right? Well it is the same for some beginners entering the complex world of the marine hobby.

So let's get started with,

What A Filter Sock Is And What Does It Do?

Filter socks have been around for a long time and have been used on both freshwater and saltwater aquariums as a form of mechanical filtration. They are normally made out of polyester or a fine mesh sown together and have a plastic ring or draw string at the top.

They are basically used like a net. They go under the return pipe and catch all the large particles of waste, food, poop etc. Filter socks vary in how big the holes in the mesh are (most commonly 200-800 microns), the bigger the holes the less they will remove. Filter socks normally rest in a holder that clips on the side of your sump wall.

Every so often (we will discuss how often next) you clean the filter sock and by doing so you are removing all these large particles of detritus and waste from your aquariums water. Most people have several filter socks and simply rotate the socks as they clean them. This means when you remove a filter sock to clean you can put on the spare straight away so your aquarium doesn't go without its mechanical filtration.

Cleaning is simple, you can use your shower, tap, tank water or washing machine. I personally used the shower (FYI – the family members using the same bathroom might dislike this!) and it removes all the muck from the sock. I then let it dry naturally and it is as good as new.

Maintenance! The Part People Make Mistakes On!

This is the reason I decided to include this section! One of my mistakes early on was not cleaning my filter sock as often as I should have. I recommend doing this ever few days depending on your bio-load.

And here is why...

Over time more and more detritus, uneaten food and livestock waste will gather in the filter sock, which is a good thing as it's what they are designed to do. However, this waste remains in the water column and continues to break down within the sock. By cleaning the filter socks every few days you are manually removing all the waste in the sock before it has a chance to break down.

If you are going to leave your filter sock in for a long time and let the waste rot in your tank then why use a filter sock at all? It's surprising how fast the filter socks become clogged with waste and detritus.

As I stated earlier, some hobbyists use them and others don't. It is completely up to you!

I would never run an aquarium without one as I have seen how dirty mine gets in just a few days. If I didn't run a filter sock all that detritus and waste would be left in my water column.

Just make sure to do one thing if you use a filter sock...

Clean them often!!

For The Beginner – No matter what media you are running (be it filter socks, filter floss or any other type of media) the key is to clean them often! If you have a sump with a filter sock then clean them every few days. If you have a back wall filter with some floss then replace the floss often.

Its that's simple.

How often you need to clean your media really depends on your bio load. If you don't have much stock then you could probably go with cleaning them only once a week. If you have a fully stocked aquarium then you will need to clean them every few days. A rule of thumb is once your media starts to look dirty, that is when you should think about cleaning it.

Uv Steriliser

(Optional)

A UV steriliser is another piece of equipment that can help you maintain a healthy aquarium. In simple terms, UV sterilizers work by passing aquarium water over an ultraviolet bulb.

The UV light kills the bacteria, algae and parasites in the water before returning it to the display aquarium. In conjunction with a quality filtration system, UV sterilizers are an excellent way to help keep your aquarium clean.

The main reason for using a UV steriliser is to keep pest algae, bacteria and parasites under control. Lack of proper maintenance in a saltwater aquarium can lead to algae or parasite blooms that can become very problematic. The use of a UV steriliser will keep such things at bay.

The only down side to using a UV steriliser is that the UV radiation is a non-discriminate killer. This basically means it will not only kill the bad bacteria but it will also kill the good bacteria. This is something you will need to think about, do the benefits out way the negatives?

If you are having problems with algae and parasites, then yes a UV steriliser is worth investing in. If you are doing fine without one then there is no real reason why you should add one to your system. It's nice to have but not essential. It's more of a personal preference among hobbyists.

For The Beginner – A UV Steriliser is not necessary for a beginner. This is more of a problem solver than a must have item. If you have serious issues with bacterial blooms and algae then this item is one of the solutions to that problem.

This section is simply to inform you of what one is.

Ro Di Unit

When mixing saltwater for your aquarium you buy the salt from a LFS but what about the water we mix it with? Do we just use tap water?

HELL NO

We use RO/DI water...

An RO/DI unit is a water purification system that any serious hobbyists will own. RO/DI stands for Reverse Osmosis/ De-Ionized which are the functions performed to purify water.

They basically filter the water to produce pure H2O with no nitrate, phosphate, metals etc. This way you know exactly what you are putting in your aquarium. RO/DI water when mixed with marine salt makes the ideal saltwater for any aquarium with the ideal parameters.

Most RO/DI units have four stages to their filtration,

Stage 1 – A sediment filter where water passes through a sponge to filter out any large particles.

Stage 2 – Water passes through an activated carbon filter. The carbon absorbs chemicals and removes the chlorine from the water.

Stage 3 – The water is purified through a membrane via reverse osmosis.

Stage 4 – The water will pass through a resin which will remove any remaining ions, it deionises the water.

In order for the RO/DI unit to filter the water properly the filter, resin and membrane need to be replaced on a regular basis. This is extra cost on top of everything else in the hobby that many hobbyists simply can't afford.

For these hobbyists there is a simple solution. Many LFS will sell RO/DI water at a very reasonable price. Simply take a water container to your LFS and they will fill it up with filtered water for around £5/$5 per 25l, which is much more affordable.

If you are setting up a Nano aquarium it's probably more cost efficient to buy filtered water from your LFS as your water changes are going to be smaller, only a couple of litres per week. If you have a large aquarium that will need large water changes and has a high evaporation rate getting an RO/DI unit might be worth your while. It will certainly make life easier as carrying 25l of water from the LFS to your car isn't easy.

For The Beginner – I would put off buying your own RO/DI Unit initially. Most beginners start off with a nano aquarium and getting water from your LFS is the easier and cheaper option.

Once you get established in the hobby and you know the basics then you can think about getting an RO/DI unit.

Dosing Unit

A dosing pump is for the more experienced hobbyist who keeps a lot of coral.

As corals grow they use up some trace elements within the water column and keeping these elements topped up is essential.

For example; corals use calcium for their skeletons. They get this calcium from the water they live in, if the calcium levels in the water drop, coral growth will be affected. Less calcium in the water means there is less for the corals to use which means the coral growth rate will slow.

To keep these levels topped up hobbyists add these elements into the water column. Many add these by hand (adding a few drops per day depending on their tanks rate of consumption) but there is a better, more reliable method.

And that comes in the form of a dosing pump. This pump will simply add a certain amount of mixture to the aquarium over the course of the day. You can set the pump to add the amounts you need and at intervals you desire.

They make life easier as it's one less thing you need to think about.

For The Beginner – This section is just an FYI. As a beginner there is no need to think about dosing just yet. Until you have a system full of corals a simple water change can maintain your waters parameters. I have had a mixed reef aquarium for years and have only recently started to dose this system.

Non-Essential Equipment

Every article, post or website will have skimmers, pumps, wave-makers etc. in their equipment sections. Which let's be honest, makes total sense. They are some of the key pieces of equipment that keep our little reefs up and running. What about the less important pieces of equipment, the ones that may not be essential but the ones that can make life that little easier?

For example;

I am talking about a simple bucket or gravel vac for your water changes. As you remove water from your aquarium and siphon it off into the bucket, you can use it to place corals, fish etc. A simple bucket is a very versatile piece of equipment for a hobbyist.

So here is a list of all the 'none essential' pieces of equipment that I use on a daily/weekly basis that you might just find useful.

Bucket

Well as I have stated it has many uses. My most resent use was to refill my auto top off unit with fresh water. But in the past is has been used to store all my fish and coral when my old tank cracked. That day it was well worth the £5 I paid for it.

Try to stay away from a metal bucket. After a while the metal will start to rust and could leech elements into the water.

Paper Towels
You can use a normal towel if you desire but something like this is needed to constantly clean the front of the aquarium from salt marks. I am forever doing this as I hate it when these marks ruin the view. I also use this to dry equipment I have used so the salt water doesn't damage it.

Turkey Baster
I only really use this to remove the detritus from a corner of my aquarium. It's the only place in my aquarium where detritus seems to build up, and a few blasts from the turkey baster gets all that waste it into the water column and into my filtration.

Note Pad
This is where I keep all my maintenance records and test results. It's a simple and cheap way for me to see trends in my test results. I use to use my laptop to keep my records but as I learned the hard way, saltwater and a laptop don't mix well.

Spare Equipment
I use my spare Heater/ Pump to help mix my saltwater for a water change and to get it to the correct temperature. It's also handy to have a spare heater/ pump in case of emergencies. My heater recently packed up and my whole aquarium could have collapsed if it wasn't for my spare heater.

Tooth Brush / Wire Brush

This is for those deep cleaning days. I normally use a toothbrush for my cleaning my skimmer. It's one of the best ways to clean those dirty corners and hard to react places.

Net

For obvious reasons when buying a new fish I don't like to add any of the LFS's water to my reef tank. A net also comes in handy when you need to remove a fish or invert for whatever reason.

Sand Bed Siphon/ Gravel Vacuum

This is something everyone needs if they have a sand bed. They are relatively inexpensive and make cleaning your sand bed and performing your water changes easy.

Glass Scraper (Algae Remover)

This is something every hobbyist out there has to do from time to time. Be it algae, coralline growth or other critters growing on the glass of the aquarium, they all have to go!

They all spoil the view to our reef and make our aquarium look (for lack of a better word) 'unclean'. We put so much effort into our aquariums to make them look beautiful it's a shame when we can't see them in all their beauty because of unclean glass.

Luckily enough it's easy to clean and almost every LFS stock glass scrapers that clean the glass. The only thing you need to worry about is scratching the glass surface.

This is also simple enough to prevent as all you need to do is to take care when cleaning the glass. Try not to rush when cleaning and try not to go to close to the sand bed as sand particles stuck under the scraper can cause damage to the glass.

TIP – One way to prevent scratching the tank is to maintain the glass scraper blade. If the scraper looks damaged, it may in fact cause damage to your glass. Many glass cleaners come with replaceable blades to make this process easier. Those scrapers that don't come with replacements should be replaced if damaged. Your aquarium cost more than the glass scraper so don't risk damaging the walls over a relativity cheap piece of equipment.

I know it's not, but I always feel like my aquarium is dirty when the glass isn't clean. Cleaning the glass is a simple aspect of aquarium maintenance but it's a very essential one in my opinion. I love the crystal clean look of my reef after the glass has been cleaned.

That's A Lot Of Equipment Right?

Well for the most part equipment isn't cheap and the cost can soon start to climb. My advice if you are on a budget is to go second hand. Look on eBay, your LFS, craigslist or even join some local saltwater aquarium Facebook groups and see what they have to offer. A lot of the time people are selling full set ups at a really good price as they need a quick sale. This is often a great way to start the hobby as it works out a lot cheaper. So if you do eventually decide that this hobby is not for you then it isn't as big of a risk as you haven't spent as much money as you could have.

In terms of setting up equipment, well you think that would be straight forward, right?

As I found out the hard way setting up some pieces of equipment can be a lot of hassle and it can be so frustrating. This is something I didn't think about when I got my first aquarium. I opened up the box and removed my tank to find a lot of parts and equipment I knew very little about. This is something we will go into detail later on in the guide.

Q – Do I really need all this expensive equipment?

A – NO. That would be my honest opinion, and here is why,

In theory you can run a saltwater aquarium on nothing more than a sponge filter (I do not recommend this, this is in theory). A saltwater aquarium is all about balance. As long as you have an established colony of beneficial bacteria where nitrification and denitrification occurs you have the bare bones of the filtration needed. All you need is to ensure you have the correct lighting and flow required for your livestock and you have everything you need for a basic saltwater aquarium.

However, the more livestock you add the more waste that will enter your aquarium. As a result of this you will need to improve your methods of removing said waste. This is where people add skimmers, filter socks, roller mats, carbon etc. A lot of the time the more filtration options you are running the easier it is to maintain stable parameters.

For The Beginner - There is a wide range of equipment out there and it can get confusing. I would recommend starting out with the basics. You will need a heater or chiller for temperature control and a return pump for your filtration with some form of filter floss or filter sock. A good light is needed for corals and if your aquarium water looks to calm then you may need to add a wave maker.

That's about it initially. A filter sock/floss, a return pump, a heater or chiller and a wave maker will be a good start. Combine that with some biological filter media and you are good to go. This will be enough to keep a few fish and some basic corals. More equipment can easily be added at a later date.

Now that we have a rough idea of what equipment goes into our tanks, let's have a look at the décor for the display tank. The next few steps are all about setting up your aquarium. We will start by adding rock, substrate and water.

Step 4a

Décor
Substrate or Bare Bottom?

Every saltwater aquarium is different and personal to the creator. As a result of this we (as hobbyists) have a vast range of aquariums that all look unique. Some people go for a more natural appearance and others aim for a simplistic look. There is no wrong way of setting up your aquarium as it's your choice!

One of the first things you will need to decide on is are you going bare bottom or using substrate.

Within this section I am simply going to list the pros and cons of going bare bottom or using substrate. I am not necessarily going to recommend a specific one as I believe that is up to you.

Silly Question – What does bare bottom and substrate mean?

Answer – Bare bottom simply means having no sand or gravel in your aquarium. Substrate is what you put on the base of your aquarium, such as sand or gravel.

Easily answered right? See the importance of asking those silly questions? They are often a simple and easy answer that is helpful to know!

Anyway... bare bottom or substrate?

Bare-Bottom

Pros

- Gives the aquarium a clean look that many people find attractive in the modern home.

- It's easy to clean (unlike sand or gravel) as no detritus can build up and cause your parameters to spike.

- In no time coralline algae will grow over the glass base giving a clean looking base to the aquarium. Others also use coral to grow over the base of their aquarium.

Cons

- The bare bottom can be an unnatural look to the aquarium that many dislike.

- Many inverts, fish and marine critters like to live in the substrate; these animals are now off limits in your aquarium.

- Substrate like crushed coral can buffer the pH and Hardness of the water keeping constant and stable water chemistry. Bare bottom = no substrate.

Substrate

Pros

- Substrate gives the aquarium a natural look that many aim to have.

- The use of sand, crushed coral or gravel is the home of many marine aquarium inhabitants that you can keep happy and healthy.

- As previously stated, the use of substrate and help buffer the pH and Hardness of your water chemistry, helping to maintain a stable environment.

- Acts as a base support for live rock to be mounted on. If your rock formation falls apart, the rock will land on the sand bed. With no sand bed the rock will land on the glass base of the aquarium with risk of chipping the glass.

Cons

- Nitrate, Gases, Ammonia, Nitrite, etc. can often build up in a sand bed and once disturbed gasses are released becoming toxic and raise parameters within your aquarium.

- Cleaning can sometimes become hard work. Detritus can build up within a sand bed quickly and a structured cleaning schedule needs to be put in place.

- Often looks messy and many critters and fish move the sand bed around on a regular basis, resulting in mounds of sand and rock formations being moved around.

Like I said it's entirely up to you what you use within your aquarium. Often the type of aquarium you are wanting will directly affect your choice in substrate. I personally have a shallow sand bed that is around 1-2cm deep. It's enough for my critters to live in and keeps my goby happy. Cleaning is simple as the sand bed isn't deep and most of my inverts turn over the sand bed on a regular basis. This is my personal choice.

Aquariums with both bare-bottom and substrate can look amazing and house both fish and corals. It's up to you to weigh up the pro's and con's of both and make your decision.

Things to think about;

- What type of aquarium do you want to have?

- What fish and inverts do you want to keep?

- Natural look or clean and modern?

Once you answer these questions you will have a rough idea of what you require. Put your answers against the pros and cons of each to see what matches up the best. The best fit is what you should go for.

For The Beginner – To begin with I would suggest going with a shallow crushed coral sand bed. This will be easy enough to clean for a beginner and give the aquarium a nice natural feel. If you later on decide you want to go bare bottom. Then simply remove the sand bed bit by bit.

Substrate size (how big the grains of sand are) isn't a huge issue. I would simply go for one that you like the look of.

Step 4b

Décor

Rock

The building blocks of any successful aquarium are the rocks within it. It doesn't matter if this started out as live rock, dry natural rock or man-made rock, rock of some kind is needed in a saltwater tank (again, to some degree. You can technically run a saltwater aquarium with no rock, and it will work but I tend not to recommend this). It provides fish with hiding places, a mount for coral placement and much more.

Live rock was once primarily used as the filtration media of a saltwater aquarium. The rock provides plenty of surface area for bacteria to populate, multiply and process all the leftover food and waste in the aquarium. This is an essential aspect of any reef aquarium and the rock plays a crucial part in the nitrogen cycle. As the hobby has advanced live rock is no longer relied upon for its bacteria benefits. Instead media designed primarily to house bacteria is more widely used within the hobby today.

'Live Rock' by definition is not rock that gets up and moves around (sorry if you got excited about that). The 'live' part of live rock simply refers to the life on and within the rock (bacteria, algae and small critters) that will grow and multiply within your aquarium. 'Dead Rock' is simply the opposite; it is dry rock with no aquatic life living on or in it. It's your choice which one you go with.

Live Rock

Live rock tends to be fragmented pieces of old coral reef that broke off during storms or by wave movements.

These pieces then wash into shallower water where they are naturally colonised by marine life such as invertebrates, corals, sponges, and millions of beneficial nitrifying bacteria. Dry rock can become live overtime as creatures and bacteria start to colonise the rock.

Pros.

Beneficial Bacteria
Most live rock is already seeded with beneficial bacteria that can process ammonia into nitrite and then nitrate. As a result of this the initial tank cycle is much faster than if you were using dry rock.

Hitch Hikers
For the most part this is a huge problem with live rock but not all of these critters are bad. Some of them are a great part of the clean-up crew and are beneficial to a reef. It all comes down to pot luck.

Cons

Hitch Hikers
The one big downside to live rock is that you never know what

you are truly putting into your aquarium. You never know what lies inside so there is always the possibility of introducing some unwanted critters such as a mantis shrimp or a crab that might munch on coral.

Anemones such as Aptasia or Majano can also be attached to live rock and cause major problems since they are capable of spreading quickly and overtaking an entire reef. Problematic algae such as bryopsis or hair algae are other potential hitch hikers that can bring reef keepers to their knees.

Cost
Live rock tends to be one of the most expensive types of rock available in most shops. If you have a large aquarium that needs filling, this could be an unexpected cost.

Dry Rock

Dry rock is exactly the same as live rock but dry and has no aquatic live on or within the rock structure.

There are two main types of dry rock, natural and man-made.

Man-made (such as real reef rock) has recently become very popular in the hobby. It's cheaper in price and has no ill effect on the oceans natural reefs. Conservation is a key concern for many reefers and man-made rock offers a great alternative to using rock harvested from the oceans. It has been created and designed with aquariums in mind making it an ideal option for any reef aquarium.

Pros

Easy to Scape

As it's dry you can play around with your scape outside of the water. There is no mess, it's easy to putty or glue together as it isn't submerged in water and you can change your scape as often as you desire with no consequences.

Cost

Dry rock is reasonably priced and tends to be more readily available in most shops. If you are ordering online dry rock is very easily shipped.

No Hitch Hikers

You get full control over what goes into your aquarium and you won't have any unwanted guests making their way in.

Cons

Longer to Cycle

As for dry rock, it can take longer to cycle if you don't seed the biological bed with nitrifying bacteria so more patience is sometimes necessary. You also lose the benefits associated with having coralline algae, although you can add it via coralline scrapings from another aquarium or a commercial starter kit.

An additional downside with dry rock is the possibility it might leach phosphates into the water, which could spur on algae growth. One way to get around this is to remove the phosphates by giving the rock a bath in an acid solution. Phosphate coming from dry rock is very rare and I have never seen it happen myself, only heard stories of it so I wouldn't worry too much about this.

Tip - From experience dry rock is much easier to scape. This can be done outside of the aquarium and you can play with the layout as much as you want. The layout is something you are going to have to be happy with for a long time, as once it is glued together the only way to rearrange it is to smash it up. If you are a perfectionist then go with dry rock and you can perfect the layout with ease.

The best thing to do is get a paper/cardboard cut-out of the aquarium size, and play with your rock on there It's the easiest way to create your ideal scape with no risk of falling rocks scratching or damaging your aquarium.

Overall it comes down to your personal choice. I started my own aquarium of with live rock (and have had great success) but as I have some pest critters for my next aquarium I will be using dry natural reef rock. I have seen many amazing reef aquariums set up from all kinds of rock. Basically there is no wrong option and truthfully it makes little difference in the long run as to what rock you start out with.

Do some research, ask around and chose what is best for you.

For The Beginner – I would go with dry rock for your first aquarium. This gives you a good chance to play around with the scape outside of the aquarium. It also limits your initial risk of getting unwanted critters and having to deal with them. Real reef rock is a good option but any dry rock designed for saltwater aquariums will work just fine.

So, by now hopefully you have a rough idea of what rock/ substrate you are going to be putting in your aquarium. Which means just one thing, it's time to scape!

Step 4c

Rock Scape

This tends to be the part people spend hours trying to create the perfect rock scape for their little reef.

Now some people out there will simply drop the rock in and it will look perfect but for most of us mere mortals (myself included) it's not that simple. Most of my first attempts ended up in rage and frustration rather than the layout I wanted.

You see, I struggled to get the rocks in the aquarium to match the picture in my head (of how I wanted my aquarium to look). Obviously the laws of physics didn't apply to my imagination.

After a few days of getting nowhere I did some research (on Google, you know, like everyone else does) and I found out that there is not just one way to scape an aquarium, there are bloody loads. I simply found one I liked and tried to recreate it. Doing your own research is key to your success within this hobby.

But I will provide a few tips that might help you out...

TIP 1

After a few months of adding corals here and there my rock scape changed dramatically, so if you are not happy with your 'beginning layout' I wouldn't worry too much as in time it will most likely change.

TIP 2

It's important when structuring your rock to make the structures as open as possible and leave space behind the rock for water flow to pass. Try not to stack huge sections against the glass or weirs as the water flow can't easily pass behind them. This area of still calm water where there is little flow is known as a dead spot.

TIP 3

It will never be perfect! There are probably aspects of every hobbyist's aquarium that they are not too keen on. If you want a successful aquarium then you are going to have to learn not to meddle with the rock structure on a regular basis. This isn't healthy for your reef and can stress the livestock causing illness or death. Remember, nature isn't perfect and it still looks beautiful.

TIP 4

Take into consideration the type of livestock that you are intending to keep. If you want large fish such as tangs then you are going to need an open water aquarium as these fish love to swim. On the other hand if you are going to keep eels and smaller fish then having a rock structure that has caves and hiding places is a good idea.

TIP 5

Utilize all of your tank space. When setting up your rock work don't just keep it all at one level. Ideally you want a mixture of heights within your aquarium. Try setting up some taller levels/columns alongside your lower base levels. This is beneficial for corals as some prefer more light than others. Higher up in your aquarium and closer to the light source means corals have access to a higher intensity of light. Lower down and future away from the light source means the corals receive less light.

TIP 6

Avoid making one big pile of rocks in the middle of the aquarium. This causes far too many dead spots within the structure where food, fish waste and detritus will collect and in turn rot. If you also need to remove a fish/invert (for whatever reason) it is very difficult. If a fish dies in your aquarium and is in the middle of the rock structure there is only one way to get it out and that is to take apart your whole scape. If you design a layout that is open enough it makes getting access to your livestock (or not so livestock depending on its current condition) much easier.

Tip 7

Always set up your rock structure and then add your substrate. This ensures the rock is sturdy on the base of the aquarium. If the rocks are simply placed on a sand bed, if the sand moves the rocks move.

In the end it all comes down to one thing. The fact it is your own aquarium and the layout you choose is your own design. Of course you need to think about the practicality of your layout (being open, allowing good flow, etc.) but you also need to create something that you personally like as you will be the one looking at your creation on a daily basis.

For The Beginner – Go out and buy some rocks you like the look of. Have a play in the shop to see what you think would work well.

When you get home and start to play with your rock scape you may benefit from smashing some of the big rocks up. This gives you more rocks to play with and using some glue or reef putty you can stick them together to form the shapes you want.

Always use a reef safe glue or putty (that you can buy in most LFS) when sticking rocks together.

Try not to overthink the scape and keep it simple.

Step 5

Adding Water

This is generally done in one of two ways. Which way depends on what type of rock/sand you are going to be using in your aquarium.

Step 5a

Dry Rock and Dry Sand

If you are using dry rock (such as real reef rock or dead coral bones) then this method is for you.

To begin with give the rock and sand a good wash in tap water/ RO/DI to remove dust and other bits that you don't want in your aquarium. Many people soak their rock/sand in water prior to adding it to their aquarium but this part is optional. As long as you give them a good clean you will be fine.

Carefully place your rock in your aquarium and create the aquascape you desire (4c). Then gently add a layer of sand into your aquarium and level it out.

Tip – Make sure the rock base is under the sand and make sure it's sturdy. The last thing you want is your final scape falling over when the flow kicks in.

If needed, use a reef safe putty or super glue to adhere the rocks together and maintain the structure you desire. This will add support to your rock scape. If using super glue/gel make sure it can be used in an aquarium (normally I ask other hobbyist to see if they have used it in the past with no ill effect but super gels are generally better than super glues).

Then simply add your salt water (5c) to your aquarium once your rock scape is set.

Step 5b

Live Rock and Live Sand

If you are adding live rock and sand it's a little different than the dry rock/sand method. Live rock is full of critters and bacteria that if left out of the water for too long will die off (not what you want!). To avoid this you will need to add the saltwater to your aquarium first (5c). Once the water is at the desired temperature (25 degree) and your salinity level (1.026) is stable you can gently add your sand and set out your live rock structure (4c).

Reef safe putty can be used underwater but don't over handle it as it will cloud surrounding water very easy. Putty is a great way to add strength to any reef scape.

Tip - Run your aquarium for a day or two with the saltwater in and then go and buy your live rock. This way you can add it straight into your aquarium minimising the loss of live on your rock.

Step 5c

Saltwater

So you have begun step 5a and 5b and arrived here.

It's now time to add your saltwater to your aquarium. There are normally two ways to obtain your saltwater;

Fresh Sea Water

This one is easy if you live near the sea front. Simply take some containers down to the sea and get the amount of water you need.

Many hobbyists simply warm the water up and add it straight to their aquariums with no/minimal filtration.

Those who are more cautious tend to run the water through a filter sock before they add it to their tank.

All you need to do is let the water settle within your container overnight. This will not only allow the water to warm up to room temperature but it will also allow all the sediment to settle on the bottom of the container. Then simply pour in the water but make sure you leave the last 5-10% of water in the container to prevent all the sediment form entering your aquarium.

There is some negativity towards to use of natural sea water in the home aquarium within the reefing community. Possibly due to the fact it isn't the 'common' method of choice. Many hobbyists swear by the use of natural sea water and often claim that since they have started to use it they have seen a significant increase in their coral health and growth.

It's free and easy to collect (providing you live near the coast or drive) so it's ideal for many hobbyists on a budget.

But for the majority of hobbyists out there, there is only one way to get the perfect saltwater for your reef...

Mixing Your Own Saltwater

This method is probably the most common way to make your saltwater, and it's so simple!

All you need to do is mix your RO/DI water with your chosen salt mix.

DO NOT USE TABLE SALT! This is not the salt you need! It may be fine on fish and chips but is not great in a reef tank! You need to use aquarium reef salt designed for the hobby.

Every reef salt has guidance on the ratio of salt to water to produce the ideal salinity (1.025-1.026). I recommend you do your own research on types of salt and see which one is best for you.

Check out their reviews on shopping sites, see what local reefers are using/ recommend via social media groups and visiting your LFS to see what types of salt mixes are on offer near you.

Tip - Add the RO/DI water to your empty tank (or dry rock scape) and then add the amount of salt in your sump (or tank) and turn on your flow. This will naturally mix the salt and water in a few hours. Then use a refractor to test your salinity level. If it's too high, add more fresh RO/DI water. If it's too low, add more salt.

Whether you use natural sea water or synthetic salt mixes it makes little difference overall. Both have been used in many types of aquariums with success.

As with everything in this hobby, ultimately it comes down to your personal preference.

For The Beginner – My recommendation for the beginner is to use a synthetic salt mix such as quantum, red sea, fluval etc. This is the easiest method and every LFS that stock marine livestock will have some form of salt available.

Which salt you chose tends to come down to which one you can easily get a hold of. I have yet to hear of a bad salt mix from a known brand. I have used many makes over the years and I haven't really noticed any difference. All I would suggest is to stick with a popular and known brand.

Step 6 – Changing Your Scape

To some this is a pointless step and you can go ahead and skip it if you see fit. But if you are like me and always change your mind on how you want your rocks positioned, or where you want your power head to be placed etc. then this step is for you.

Take some time and look at your aquarium to see if the rock structure is ideal for your choice of inhabitants. It's easier to change things around with no livestock in your aquarium as you don't worry about crushing coral or fish.

Tip - Ensure the rock work is away from the front and sides of the tank as you will need to clean these on a regular basis. So getting to them is a must unless you like the look of algae.

Tip - Think of flow in your tank, you don't want there to be any dead spots in the aquarium where waste will build up.

Tip – Refer back to step 4c if needed.

For The Beginner – By this point you should have your aquarium full of water and your rock scape set up. This is your initial set up. Your next task is to maintain it!

Step 7a
The Nitrogen Cycle

The nitrogen cycle within a marine aquarium is essential for saltwater success as it's the biological filtration of your aquarium. It's a chain reaction that results in the birth of various types of nitrifying bacteria that ultimately turn ammonia into nitrate.

There are three components involved in this process. They are ammonia, nitrite and nitrate. I'm sure you will have heard of these before?

Well if you come from the freshwater hobby you will have. If not don't panic, it's easy to get your head around!

In general the nitrogen cycling process usually takes about 30 days, but there is no exact time frame as each aquarium is different and many factors influence the cycle.

Testing your aquariums water during the cycle is very important as this will tell you what stage of the cycle you are going through at the time of the test.

Stage 1 – Ammonia

The first component in the nitrogen cycle is ammonia. This is the only time that ammonia should be present within the aquarium.

It's only once ammonia begins to build up within the aquarium that the cycling process begins.

Ammonia is produced by fish and other livestocks waste, excess food and decaying organic matter from both animals and plants. Using livestock for the purpose of cycling is not easy as they are exposed to highly toxic levels of ammonia and nitrite during the cycling process.

As a result of this many hobbyists drop some food into the aquarium to kick start the cycle. As the food decays ammonia is produced and the cycling process can begin.

This is the only time in your aquariums life span that it is difficult to get ammonia! Honestly, these little fish love to poop!

Anyway...

About ten days into the cycle the nitrifying bacteria will convert the ammonia into Nitrite.

Stage 2 – Nitrite

Just like ammonia, nitrite can be toxic and harmful to livestock even at low levels. Nitrite will continue to rise to high levels throughout the cycle. At around day 25 the levels should begin to lower (although it is possible for this phase of the cycle to last a lot longer). By day 30 the nitrite levels should be close to 0. If not don't worry as like I said this part of the phase can sometimes take a bit longer.

Now that the ammonia has been cycled into nitrite, the nitrite in turn is cycled into nitrate.

Stage 3 – Nitrate

The third and final nitrifying bacteria are living entities that require oxygen and food (an ammonia source) to survive. They grow on every surface within the tank and as they consume ammonia, nitrate is produced.

When the nitrate readings begin to increase you can tell these beneficial nitrifying bacteria are starting to establish themselves. This is the end goal of the cycle so when you start to notice these higher levels of nitrate the cycle is coming to an end.

Although nitrate is less toxic than ammonia and nitrite you still don't want high levels of it. Controlling nitrate can be done in many ways form water changes, to keeping algae in a refugium or through the process of denitrification. It tends to be a personal choice of which method you choose as different ones suit different reefers.

For The Beginner - This is a very important aspect of any aquarium. This process is your biological filtration.

Step 7b

Patience

This is the step many people skip and learn the hard way that they should have just took their time. I personally made this mistake with my first aquarium and it was costly in both time and money. Although this step ties in with the previous section many people tend to lack the necessary patience's needed to be successful within this hobby.

You need to let your aquarium cycle and allow the bacteria to grow and take hold. You will most likely see brown algae (Diatoms) on the sand and rock surface but this is normal and it normally goes away on its own once the cycle has finished.

You will get spikes in your parameters within this stage and again this is completely normal. These will settle down as the cycle progresses. Just remember to be patient.

Tip - *Use this time to research what fish, coral and/or inverts you are wanting. What fish can live in what community, their fully grown size, their diet etc. This is the section where most beginners fail. Patience is a must.*

Step 8

Test Time

So you are still waiting for your tank to finish its cycle or you think the cycle is near its end and are getting impatient.

Well there is only one way to find out if your tank is ready for its first inhabitants and that is by testing your parameters.

Using a test kit (RedSea kits are what I use, but there are a wide range of makes and models you could use) follow the instruction provided and test each parameter. Each different test kit has its own set of specific instructions so always follow the instructions designed for its own particular make of test kit.

There are a range of parameters that you will need to test and each have their own ideal level for a marine aquarium. Take a look at 'step 10b- Test Time - Test Kits' for more information on water parameters and which ones you will need to test.

Tip - Use excel or a notepad to keep a record of your test results, this way you can see trends and spikes with ease. This will help you out in the long run when you inevitably experience some issues. Keep track of your test results can give you an idea of what is causing the problem within your system (If you experience any that is). If you desire you can also use our log book – Reef-fins saltwater aquarium maintenance log book.

Testing your parameters is the easy part; the hard part is

keeping them stable. This is the one and only real challenge hobbyists face on a daily basis. Those who keep their parameters stable are the ones with beautiful reef tanks (As after all, we do not keep coral or fish, we keep water).

Go to *'Step 10b – How to Keep Your Parameters Stable for more information'*.

For The Beginner – Testing takes times to get the hang of. Simply follow the instructions carefully each time and you will be fine. Step 10b will help. I go into detail about testing and parameters within this step. To avoid repeating myself and making this book longer than it needs to be I have only went into detail once. So jump ahead to step 10b and then come right back!

Step 9

Adding Livestock

Finally! This is the moment most people look forward to.

So your aquarium is all set up. All your parameters are at a good level and your aquarium has been fully cycled. You have set your aqua-scape over and over again until you are happy with it and now it's finally time to get some creatures in your system.

You can start with any fish or invert you desire, however I would fully recommend picking a hardy, cheaper critter. Your aquarium is newly set up and there could potential be problems that may cause stress to your fish/invert or even death.

It's for this reason that it's recommended by many hobbyists that you get a hardy fish/invert that can handle the harsher condition of a newly set up aquarium.

The first livestock many hobbyists start with tends to be the clean-up crew critters.

For The Beginner – I fully recommend you start out with your clean-up crew. Hermit crabs, cleaner shrimps and turbo snails are some of the best livestock to add to your new aquarium. Hermit crabs are what I started off with.

Step 9a

Clean-Up Crew

The first livestock many hobbyists add to their aquarium tends to be the clean-up crew.

Why?

Overtime uneaten food, waste and algae often build up in an aquarium and unless you are personally going to improve your maintenance schedule then I recommend you get some help to overcome this issue.

This is where your clean-up crew comes into action. When I say clean-up crew I don't mean a team of maids come charging in and give everything a deep clean.

Instead you get round the clock care performed by hard working little critters that will munch their way through left over food and unsightly algae. Sounds good right? Well here are a few things you need to know about the critters involved in this necessary team.

I personally would be lost without the little team I have. They aren't the prettiest of creatures but if you are trying to create a sustainable ecosystem then they are going to come in handy.

We can only do so much in terms of maintenance and often need help from Mother Nature. The creatures involved in the clean-up crew often come in the form of shrimps, crabs, snails, star fish and urchins (and sometimes fish). Some are reef safe, others depend on the individual critter, some are great for a newly set up aquarium and others need a mature system.

On the next few pages you will find a list of critters that are often used as part of a clean-up crew, many of which I personally use in my own aquariums. The list below is simply a good choice of critters that are commonly used.

Shrimps

Shrimps are a personal favourite of mine, they come in many forms and all do similar jobs within the aquarium. They will eat pest critters and keep their numbers under control. They will also scavenge on any leftover food preventing it from rotting at the bottom of the aquarium. As an added bonus many shrimps are reef safe.

I have listed some of the most common shrimps used within the hobby;

Peppermint Shrimp

The peppermint shrimp is part of the 'cleaner' shrimp family and often considered more of a scavenger than a cleaner. These shrimps will tend to move around the aquarium eating left over food or smaller critters found in the aquarium. It's for this reason they are a great part of any CUC.

A true peppermint shrimp may also eat glass anemone however this tends to depend on the individual shrimp. Some may eat them like they are going out of fashion and others won't even touch them. With a lot of hobbyists it tends to be pot luck.

Care level – Providing your water parameters are stable. Easy.

Temperament – Peaceful. May eat smaller shrimps and inverts.

Reef Safe – Yes.

Size – 0.5 – 1.25 Inches.

Banded Coral Shrimp / Boxing Shrimp

The Banded Coral Shrimp is often a shy shrimp that tends to hide within the rock work for up to 1 - 2 days at a time (unless you have mine that hides for weeks at a time). These shrimp should be kept on their own or as a mated pair as they will become aggressive towards other Banded coral shrimps. Larger shrimps are likely to kill smaller inverts within the aquarium but prove peaceful towards fish and corals. These shrimp tend to be intolerant to high levels of copper and nitrates so a mature aquarium tends to be better to house this individual.

Somewhere within my aquarium is a boxing shrimp. I think I see it once a month at most as it always hides under the rock work. So if you want a shrimp that you are going to see on a regular basis, a boxing shrimp might not be for you. Instead try a cleaner shrimp!

Care level – Easy. If your water parameters are stable.

Temperament – Semi-aggressive towards other inverts of a smaller size.

Reef Safe. Yes.

Size – 3 Inches. Although they appear much bigger due to their large front legs.

Cleaner Shrimp

The cleaner shrimp is possibly my favourite of all the shrimps. They are peaceful, beautiful and serve as a great part of any clean-up crew. They are considered the medic of the reef as they will remove parasites from many fish. Like all inverts the cleaner shrimp is intolerant of copper based medicines or high nitrate levels.

If you want a peaceful shrimp that rarely hides then this shrimp is for you.

Care level – Easy.

Temperament – Peaceful.

Size – 3 – 5 Inches.

Crabs

Crabs are an interesting addition to any aquarium and are often full of personality. Many crabs will often pray on fish and pick at corals. Therefore been able to identify the type of crab you have in your aquarium is a must.

Not all crabs are a pest; some can be helpful within the aquarium and prove to be a valuable member of a clean-up crew.

Emerald Crab

This hardy little crab will eat many forms of algae and other meaty items within the aquarium. I have had these little crabs for years and they are great little scavengers eating all forms of uneaten food. As an added treat they will take many forms of frozen food and often love a bit of seaweed.

Caution must be shown as there have been cases of these crabs picking at coral. I have never had a problem with the two I had but they were fed on a regular basis.

Care level – Easy . May be eaten by predatory fish.

Temperament – Semi-aggressive.

Reef Safe – With Caution. Some hobbyists have claimed that these crabs pick at corals and predate on small fish.

Size – 2.5 Inches.

Blue Legged Hermit Crab

The Blue Leg Hermit Crab is a small crab that is one of the most commonly used critters as part of the clean-up crew. As hermit crabs do, they live in the shells of snails and move to a bigger shell as they grow. If there are no empty shells within the aquarium they may kill snails to obtain a new home. If you are going to keep hermits and snails together then I recommend you keep empty shells within your aquarium.

Care level – Easy.

Temperament – Peaceful.

Reef Safe – Yes - If starved they may eat corals.

Size – 1 Inch.

Red Legged Hermit Crab

The Red Legged Hermit Crab is basically the bigger form of the Blue Hermit. They have basically the same needs and do virtually the same job within the aquarium.

Care level – Easy.

Temperament – Peaceful.

Reef Safe – Yes. If starved they may eat corals.

Size – 1.5 Inches.

Snails

Snails are commonly used within a clean-up crew and all have their own functions within the aquarium. Some spend all of their time grazing on algae on the rock work and glass while some spend their time within the substrate searching for leftover food and other meaty items. The best option is to keep a selection of snails within the aquarium that will eat algae, disturb the substrate and scavenge on leftover food.

Turbo Snail

As the name indicates these snails don't move at a snail's pace. Well, they aren't exactly fast but for a snail they can move. They love nothing more than grazing on algae within the aquarium. The correct amount of snails in your aquarium will maintain algae and prevent potential algae blooms. There are many types of turbo snails from the Mexican Turbo to the Giant Turbo but they all do the similar role within the aquarium.

Care level – Easy.

Temperament – Peaceful.

Reef Safe – Yes. However they may knock over some coral frags as they move around the tank.

Size – 0.5 – 1.5 Inches.

Nassarius Snail

The Nassarius Snail is ideal if you find your substrate is gathering muck and left over food. They bury themselves into the sand bed and scavenge for food. As a result of how they feed these snails are more suited to an established set up to where there will be enough food.

Many reefers refer to these snails as 'zombie' snails as once they detect food in the water they rise from the sand bed in their hunt just like the waking dead. Nassarius Snails work well when combined with the Turbo Snail as the combination takes care of both the sand bed and algae growth.

Care level – Easy.

Temperament – Peaceful.

Reef Safe – Yes.

Size – 0.25 – 1.5 Inches.

Cerith Snail

The Cerith snail is a small scavenger with an elongated spiral shell that is usually black with tiny white dots covering the entire shell. One of the most ideal scavengers, detritus eaters, and algae eaters these snails are perfect for the reef aquarium.

Care level – Easy.

Temperament – Peaceful.

Reef Safe – Yes.

Size - < 3 Inches.

Starfish

Starfish can be a great part of a clean-up crew but only in a mature aquarium as they need plenty of organisms to feed upon. They do a great job of scavenging detritus and uneaten food that would otherwise rot. Below are a few species of starfish that are ideal in the home aquarium.

Brittle Star Fish

Brittle Starfish are often found on live rock as a hitchhiker and are found within many aquariums. There are many forms of Brittle starfish that range in size and all are a great addition to the aquariums clean-up crew.

Brittle stars are nocturnal and often hide under rocks during the day. At night, they come out to eat detritus and small organisms. They can't tolerate copper-based medications.

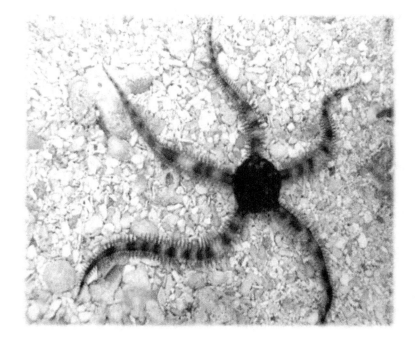

Care level – Easy.

Temperament – Peaceful.

Reef Safe – Yes.

Size – 2 – 10 Inches. Depending on type of brittle star.

Sand Sifting Starfish

These relatively bland looking creatures are bottom dwelling scavengers. They roam around the aquariums substrate eating detritus and uneaten food and are a great addition to any mature aquarium. At first glance they seem bland and colourless but at a closer inspection they have wonderful brown and beige markings. They are great for turning over the aquariums sand bed.

These Star fish are not for the newly set up aquarium. Many starfish eat micro fauna and critters that live in the sand bed and rock work of a reef tank. There simply isn't enough food for a starfish to survive in a new aquarium.

Care level – Easy. If placed in a mature aquarium with a mature sand bed so they don't starve.

Temperament – Peaceful.

Reef Safe – Yes.

Size – 12 Inches.

Other

There are several other critters that can be recruited as part of your aquariums clean-up crew. Here are a few examples of some that you may find in your local fish store.

Pincushion Urchin

The Pincushion Urchin has an oval body covered with hundreds of uniform spines. Its colour can range from red to purple to white and blue.

It requires ample hiding places and sufficient room in which to forage in the home aquarium. They are ideal at grazing on algae and clearing up left over food and detritus, although some may prey on smaller inverts within the aquarium.

Care level – Easy.

Temperament – Peaceful.

Reef Safe – Yes.

Size – 8 Inches.

Spiny Urchin

The Spiny Urchin does the same job as the Pincushion Urchin in terms of a clean-up crew. The main difference is the length of the spines on the urchin's body. These urchins are unique and look great in an aquarium.

Due to the large spines they need a larger aquarium with room to move about to prevent them breaking. Boisterous fish sometimes pierce themselves on the urchin's spines and for this reason they are best suited to a peaceful communal aquarium.

Care level – Easy.

Temperament – Peaceful.

Reef Safe – Yes.

Size – 12 Inches.

Fighting Conch

They are excellent sand sifters, and very beneficial in the reef aquarium. As they burrow and dig through the aquarium substrate, they clean and aerate the sand bed. They are very similar to snails but are on a much larger scale.

Care level – Easy.

Temperament – Peaceful.

Reef Safe – Yes.

Size – 3 + Inches.

Sea Cucumber

It does well in a large aquarium if provided with ample room to roam. Generally, for every 3 inches of sea cucumber there should be 20 gallons of water. It prefers a thick sandy substrate so it can scour through the sand for organic foods.

Like all cucumbers there is a chance they can poison an aquarium. Although it is rare, if the animal gets sucked up into a power head there is a good chance your aquarium may suffer. It is for this reason that I do not recommend them for the beginner. I am simply mentioning them to inform you of what they are.

Care level – Easy. if placed in a mature aquarium.

Temperament – Peaceful.

Reef Safe – Yes.

Size – 12 Inches.

Whatever type of clean-up crew you want to have in your aquarium you must remember not to over populate your system. Too many critters and there won't be enough food for them to eat. Many people over populate with the theory that more cleaners are better but this simply is not the case.

TIP – *Always start off with fewer critters than you think you need. If it turns out that you need more simply add them gradually. Doing it this way means you will eventually find the perfect number of critters that your tank can support.*

For The Beginner – I would start out with a few hermit crabs, one shrimp and a collection of snails. This is the basic clean-up crew found within many aquariums.

Step 9b

Fish

So it's finally time to get some fish in your system. But there are so many fish out there? Which one do you choose? What is the best fish for your tank?

Well, here is my advice and I hope it helps.

Ever since I can remember beginners have gone with the same type of fish as their starter fish, and that is the Damsel fish. These fish are beautiful and hardy which is probably the main reason why they are such a popular choice with beginners. But a short time after, as more fish are added to the aquarium, problems start to arise and people start asking themselves "Why did I choose this fish!"

Now I'm not saying all damsels are bad as many are a great fish for beginners. The problem arises when beginners choose certain types of damsels that are very aggressive and territorial when they grow. This is normally down to a lack of research on the fish and the fact most damsels are relatively inexpensive.

Here is a basic list of the peaceful and more aggressive types of damsels that are quite common in most LFS. Aggressive damsels are not bad fish, it's simply their nature and the mistake is on the hobbyists placing them in a peaceful aquarium expecting them to change. We need to work with the nature of our fish and not against it.

Damsels to Avoid

Three/Four strip damsel

Domino Damsel

Blue Devils

Yellow tail Damsel (hit and miss)

Like I said, these are not bad fish, it's simply in their nature to be territorial and therefore aggressive. When young, most are cute and brightly coloured but as they grow many tend to lose their coloration and turn dull. If you want a peaceful communal aquarium then I would recommend staying away from these fish.

TRUST ME.

In my second aquarium I purchased a four strip damsel fish as they look interesting and are a very active fish. At first it worked well and settled in great. This did not last long. Soon after the fish settled in, all hell broke out and the little damsel started to harasses and stress out all my other fish. Until all I was left with was a shy clown and a proud damsel.

Damsels Ideal for Beginners

Blue Chromis

Green Chromis

Talbot's Damsel

My personal recommendation is the Green/Blue Chromis

(photo above). They are a peaceful communal fish that lives in a shoal. Chromis are best kept in groups of 3+ and are a very active fish adding color and movement to the community tank. They are ideal reef fish and seldom bother any other aquarium inhabitants. All in all, these guys are great for the beginner. They are relatively hardy and won't break the bank. These fish won't necessarily be the stars of the show, but they enhance any reef with their beautiful colours and shoaling patterns.

Through my own personal experience (and the reports of many others) I suggest you avoid certain types of damsel and lean towards the more peaceful communal fish such as the Blue/Green Chromis. It will mean less stress on both you and your reef inhabitants as there is nothing more annoying than trying to catch a fish in a fully stocked reef.

The key to getting livestock is research!

This must be done before purchase as some fish are peaceful, some are territorial, some are predators and others eat corals. Many also grow very large indeed.

Some people love the research and others hate it, either way if you want a successful saltwater aquarium then you are going to have to do your homework.

For The Beginner – Blue green chromis are a great fish for the newly set up aquarium but if you don't want one or are struggling to find them then go with the common clownfish.

Clownfish are now bred for the aquarium hobby and have become very hardy, little fish.

If you are setting up a nano aquarium are don't have much room for many fish, then go with clownfish as your first fish.

If you have a large aquarium and room for many fish, then start off with a shoal of blue green chromis.

Whatever fish, invert or coral you decide to keep in your aquarium it will have originated from one of two places. It will be either wild caught or captive bred.

Don't think this is important? Well think again!

Wild caught

Most of the fish that you see in your local fish store will likely have come from the worlds reefs. They are collected from all over the world's tropical seas and transported across the world for the pet trade. As fish are collected from the ocean you have access to a wide range of species that come in all shapes and sizes. Basically any fish you want you can get.

...and that is where the benefits stop.

Due to over fishing, global warming, pollution etc. the population of many species are in decline and picking fish from the reefs to be placed into the pet trade is not sustainable. As a result of this many countries are putting a stop to fish, invert and coral collections and the price of livestock collected from the ocean has gone up in recent years. Many wild caught fish often struggle to adapt to live in an aquarium and many won't live past their first year in captivity.

But for now this is how the hobby is and wild caught livestock make up majority of the fish and inverts found within the hobby. If cared for properly (by the LFS, the collectors and you) they can live a happy life within a reef aquarium. The other option is to fill your aquarium with livestock that has been captive bred (or aquaculture).

Captive bread or Aqua-cultured Livestock

As technology advances (and hobbyists become more experienced) more and more species of fish have been bred in captivity. Whether it is in large breeding aquariums or within the home aquarium captive bred fish are becoming more readily available to the average hobbyists.

As these fish can be bred anywhere around the world they tend to be a lot cheaper than wild caught ones. They also tend to be hardier and live longer in the home aquarium as (unlike wild caught fish) they do not have to adjust to life in the aquarium.

Take the common clownfish for example. Years ago these fish where wild caught and use to cost a lot more than they do now. These days nearly every clownfish within the hobby has been bred within an aquarium of some sorts.

And the best part about captive bred fish...

There is no impact on the world's reefs.

Hopefully one day all the fish found within the hobby will come from some form of breeding program but for now there are only a handful of fish that successful breed within the aquarium conditions. So most likely you will end up with a mixture of wild caught and captive bred fish.

For most this does not matter but some hobbyists out there only keep captive bred livestock and are keen conservationists. In an ideal world I would love a reef with only captive bred fish.

Whatever your preference you still need to find a place to purchase your livestock.

Local Fish Shop (LFS)

By far the most traditional method of acquiring live stock is going to a pet shop, more commonly known as your local fish store (LFS).

It's an ideal place to view, learn and examine any potential new purchases. Here you can check the health of the fish and, if you ask nicely, most LFS owners will feed the fish so you can see how well it eats frozen/ flake food. There is nothing better than buying a nice fat, healthy fish.

There are a few down sides to going to your LFS. The normal issues are; the prices tend to be higher, the variety of stock tends to be limited and getting to a shop can be challenging for some.

Some shops are the exception to the above as some LFS will become your ideal place to obtain stock. Many will order fish in if you are after something unique and most take good care of their livestock.

If you find a good LFS, you are set for life in terms of this hobby. The key is to visit as many as you have access to. You will find some poor ones and you will find some great ones. I recommend joining some aquarium Facebook groups from your area to see what shops experienced hobbyists recommend.

Key to buying fish from a shop;

- Ask to see it eat.

- Give the fish a health check.

- Health check other fish that are in the same water.

- Ask as many questions as you need.

- Do your research prior to walking into the shop, trust your own knowledge.

The World Wide Web

As everyone is shopping online these days it makes sense that you can also buy your livestock online too. This is great for those who don't have access to a good LFS. Many sites have a wide range of available stock and at relatively good prices. The only thing you will need to do is to pay extra for is delivery, obviously.

Just like picking an LFS, the key to buying fish online is to find the perfect site. Many sites may look good on your screen but there is nothing more depressing and frustrating then opening a box and finding a dead fish inside.

The best option is to see what sites other hobbyists use. These people have the knowledge and experience to guide you in the right directions.

You will find that whatever you do in this hobby, other hobbyists are always there if you need any friendly advice.

The major drawback to buying online is all you normally see is a stock photo of the livestock. You won't get to see the fish you have purchases until it arrives on your door step. Now this is not a problem if the site you are buying from has a good reputation. However I have heard of problems where people have purchased ill or dying livestock from particular sites. Although not common, it does happen and is something to think about if you are going to be buying online.

Key to buying fish online;

- Read through reviews to pick the best place.

- Check how they ship the animals to ensure they take care when doing so.

- Look for secure sites when buying online.

- Only buy from a reputable site.

Personally I would go and visit as many LFS as you can. No two are alike and they often stock different livestock so what you might find in one shop, you may not find in another. Getting to know your LFS is great as many will order in livestock at your request!

TIP – Don't take any money when you visit several shops in one day, it becomes expensive. My wallet has been hit hard by this mistake in the past. I mean, when you see a nice fish or coral you just can't help it.

As long as you get a healthy fish is doesn't really matter whether you buy it from a shop or online. What does matter is how you introduce it to your aquarium. You don't just open the bag and drop the fish straight into your tank. There is a correct process that you should follow to minimise the stress you put on your fish during its move.

Step 9c

Acclimation

The purpose of acclimation is simple; the water that the fish/inverts or corals are transported in has a different temperature, pH, salinity, and parameters than the water in your aquarium. Fish, and especially invertebrates (including corals), are very sensitive to even minor changes in the waters parameters, so proper acclimation is the key to ensuring their successful relocation.

There are two commonly used methods of acclimation within the hobby...

The Floating Bag Method

Step 1

Turn off the aquarium lights. This helps to calm the livestock and minimise the stress on the individual. It's also helpful to dim the lights in the room if the fish is in a box or paper bag. Severe stress or trauma may result from sudden exposure to bright light.

Step 2

Float the bag in your aquarium water for around 15 minutes. The purpose of this stage is to allow the temperature of the water in the bag to match that of the temperature of your aquariums water. Slow and steady wins the race as sudden changes can shock your livestock.

Step 3

After the bag has floated in the aquarium for around 15 minutes you will want to make a small cut in the top of the bag. You must ensure not to mix the water in the bag with the water in your aquarium. This could add unwanted pests and illness. There is an unwritten rule in the hobby and that is to never mix livestock/ LFS water with your own aquarium water.

One reason for this is that many LFS use copper based medicines within their fish only systems to prevent and kill disease, bacteria and/ or infections. As they stock a lot of fish at any given time a break out in disease could cost the LFS a lot of money. The copper based treatments they use are to prevent such break outs and keep the fish as healthy as possible during their time in the shop. As most inverts and some corals are sensitive to copper, this could be lethal if added to an established reef full of inverts.

Add a small cup full of your aquarium water into the bag and let it settle for around 5 minutes. Repeat this process several times until the bag is nearly full. This way the livestock will have chance to get use to your aquariums water parameters in a controlled manor. Again, this reduces the stress put on the livestock.

Tip – At this point the bag will start to sink. All you need to do is clip the bag to the side of your aquarium or pour the bag water in a bucket and repeat the above, just the same process but in a bucket and not a bag.

Step 4
Pour out half of the water in the bag and repeat step three.

Step 5
This is the final step. Using a net simply scoop up the livestock and place it into the aquarium. Once the livestock is safely in the aquarium discard the bag and the water within it.

The Drip Method

This method is considered more advanced. It's geared towards sensitive livestock but can be used for any.

For this process you will need airline tubing and you must be willing to monitor the entire process. You will also need a clean bucket designed for aquarium use only. It's recommended to acclimatize fish and inverts separate to avoid them harming one another.

Step 1
Follow step 1 and 2 from the floating bag process to acclimate the water temperature.

Step 2
Carefully empty the contents of the bags (including the water) into a bucket, making sure not to expose sensitive invertebrates to the air. Depending on the amount of water in each bag, this may require tilting the bucket at a 45 degree angle to make sure the animals are fully submerged.

Step 3
Using airline tubing, set up and run a siphon drip line from the main aquarium to each bucket. You'll need separate airline tubing for each bucket used. Tie several loose knots in the airline tubing, or use a plastic airline control valve, to regulate flow from the aquarium.

You can begin a siphon by sucking on the end of the airline tubing that you will be placing into the bucket. When water begins to flow through the tubing adjust the drip (by tightening one of the knots or adjusting the valve) to a rate of about 2 - 4 drips per second. Wait until there is a good amount of water in the bucket before moving onto step 4.

Step 4

This is the final step. Using a net simply scoop up the livestock and place it into the aquarium. Once the livestock is safely in the aquarium discard the water within the bucket.

Tip – Be patient. You should never rush the acclimation process. I know it's exciting but you must take your time.

Tip – Keep your aquarium lights off for a few hours after you have placed your livestock in the aquarium. This gives the new resident time to settle in and rest.

Tip – Keep an eye on your new resident for the next 24 hours to ensure the fish is eating well and does not show any signs of illness or stress. Fish, inverts and corals will all hide or sulk for a few days and this is natural.

Tip – Don't stress too much if your new fish is being harassed and chassed buy its other tank mates. This is just the fish finding out their own pecking order. This behaviour is common and normally subsides in a few days.

Step 10

Maintenance

I often like to refer to Murphy's Law 'Anything that can go wrong, will go wrong' when talking about the saltwater aquarium hobby. From my experience this is a very true statement. Equipment may fail, water parameters will fluctuate and Livestock may die. Sometimes these things happen and it can be frustrating and upsetting. This is why general maintenance is so important! We can't eradicate every issue or problem that will occur with our aquarium but we can minimise the chances of these things happening through essential maintenance.

For example;

Regular water testing will show us if our parameters are changing and we can correct this issue early before it becomes a problem and affects our livestock. If we didn't test our water parameters we would only know about the issue when it becomes a problem. It's our job as hobbyists to ensure we keep an eye on 'what can go wrong' (in this example, parameter swings) so we can prevent the 'will go wrong' (livestock death or illness) part of Murphy's Law. By checking parameters we can correct any minor issues early on and prevent a potential aquarium crash!

As stated above the keys to a successful, long term reef aquarium are KNOWLEDGE and MAINTENANCE! The more you plan, test and maintain you aquarium the better it will be and the healthier your livestock will be.

But what does this include? What should you be doing on a daily basis? Or even a weekly basis?

Well...

Maintaining a saltwater aquarium is a lot easier than most people think, it just takes a little bit of time, some knowledge and a few essentials. As long as you know what you need to do on a daily, weekly and monthly basis your aquarium should (remember Murphy's Law) run nice and smooth.

The bulk of this section will be split into three categories; Daily Maintenance, Weekly Maintenance and Monthly Maintenance. Everything you will need to do to maintain a beautiful coral reef!

Apart from this section below...

As there are a few things you will need to do/ know before you begin your aquarium maintenance. You will need to ensure that all of your equipment in working and tuned in properly (this section is aimed at those who have just recently set up their aquarium and haven't yet made any adjustments to their equipment) and you will need to know how to test the aquariums parameters and what parameters you will be testing (as maintaining stable parameters makes up a large part of your general maintenance).

Step 10a

How to Fine Tune Your Equipment?

Tuning equipment will mainly occur during the first few weeks of your aquariums life. This is simply because some equipment (such as a skimmer) takes time to get to the ideal setting. Once you have found that perfect setting you normally don't need to adjust that piece of equipment until it's due its deep clean.

Once you do your deep clean you simply repeat the process of tuning that piece of equipment. The more you do this the more you will learn what works best for your aquarium. As a result of this your 'tuning in' process becomes easier and quicker.

Lighting

Lighting plays a huge role in the saltwater aquarium, especially when corals (and other photosynthetic creatures) are involved. Corals need the correct amount of light to grow and remain healthy so getting that correct setting on your lighting is essential.

LED – Over the course of a few days slowly change your light intensity, lowering or increasing the intensity to suit the needs of your livestock. Try not to make any drastic or major changes as it may startle or stress the tank inhabitants.

For The Beignner – Getting the correct setting on your LED lighting can be tricky for a beginner. First off I would simply follow the instructions for the lights you have and keep that setting for a few days. If your corals start to 'sulk' it might be an idea to up or lower your light intensity. Do this slowly! Small changes over the course of a day or two tend to be the best approach. If you have a pur and par meter then use this to find out what setting you need to aim for. If you don't have one of these simply make small changes and see how your corals react.

T5 or Florescent Tube – There is no need to change the intensity of these lights as they are created to produces the necessary par and pur that photosynthetic creatures need.

Protein Skimmer

For me getting the correct setting on my skimmer was a nightmare. I followed what the instructions stated and it just kept overflowing. So I started to play around and found that there were two ways in which to change your skimmers settings.

The first is to change the water level that the skimmer is placed into. This can easily be done by placing some form of hard plastic under the skimmer to raise it out of the water or you can simply add more water into the aquarium to raise the water level in the sumps chambers.

The second method is to control the amount of water flowing through the skimmer itself. This is normally done by opening or closing the valve on the skimmer that controls the water coming out of the skimmers body. Opening the valve will lower the water level within the skimmer and closing the valve will raise the water level.

You want to aim to get the water level in the skimmer just

below the neck leading to the collection bowl. This is what many reefers recommend as it produces the most efficient skim.

Small changes make big differences when dealing with a skimmer. A small change every few days is recommended as it often takes a while for these changes to take effect. It took me a good few days/ weeks to get mine working properly when I first set up my skimmer.

For The Beginner - You either change the water level inside the skimmer or change the water level outside the skimmer. These are the two aspects that will affect your skimmer. It's that simple.

Return Pump (Sump Only)

Not all return pumps have power settings but most do. Just like many wave-makers they can be set from 10% to 100%, with 10% increases along the way. Changing the settings is as easy as a push of a button. The key is to get the perfect level of flow to suit the needs of your livestock.

If you are running more equipment from you return pump (such as reactors) then you might need to increase the flow rate to compensate.

Wave-makers

Power heads/ Wave makers are essential in a reef aquarium as they provide the necessary flow that livestock needs. The key is to get the correct amount of flow within your aquarium while eliminating dead spots.

Getting the correct flow can be done by lowering or increasing the power of the wave-maker. You want to aim for the goldilocks zone, not too much flow and not too little. This is generally done by making changes to the wave-maker and monitoring how your livestock reacts. If fish struggle to swim and corals are getting blown around, your flow is too high. If your corals aren't moving at all, you probably don't have enough flow.

Another purpose to the wave-maker is to eliminate dead spots. Now eliminating dead spots can be tricky. Look around the substrate or the bottom of your aquarium for a build-up of detritus and fish waste. All this waste gathers here because there is low flow in that one spot, known as a dead spot. Once found, you can simply move you wave-maker around the aquarium until to find the spot that prevents all dead spots.

I find that placing the wave-maker on the opposite side of your return pipe works great. Try this and leave it for a day or two. If you start to find dead spots then it might be worth while making some changes.

Step 10b

Testing Your Aquariums Water Parameters!

A saltwater test kit is as it sounds. A kit designed to test the water parameters within your aquarium. Water does not only consist of H2O. The water chemistry is made up of many other parameters.

Think of the water in your aquarium as the air in your home. The air is made up of many parameters and not just oxygen. To survive we need a stable atmosphere that we can breathe in. Imagine if there was a gas leak in your home, you can't see it in the air but in high amounts it can kill us. Well it's the same for your aquarium. If some of your water parameters spike, such as Ammonia, you can't see it in the water but it can kill your fish and coral.

Part of the general maintenance of any hobbyists is to ensure these levels do not spike and remain stable throughout your aquariums life span. This is crucial for the health of both fish and coral. We monitor these levels by testing each parameter using a specific test kit.

TIP – Parameter control is one of a hobbyist's biggest challenges! This is normally the reason for the death of livestock. So take note as a test kit will prove beneficial.

Stability is key in any saltwater aquarium. The ocean parameters stay at a very constant level as a result of the vast amount of water it holds. It rarely experiences sudden change in terms of temperature and/or parameters, as a result of this, livestock struggle with such change when in the aquarium, resulting with illness or death.

If only we had a way to monitor these parameters so we could detect a spike before it became lethal...?

Basically, you need a test kit for your aquarium for the same reason you need a carbon monoxide detector in your home. It's to keep a check on certain parameters so they don't spike and harm the livestock. You wouldn't risk not having a carbon monoxide detector in your home because you thought it would be fine and the fact your air 'looked' clean? So why do it for your aquarium?

If you are serious about creating a part of the ocean within your very own home or having an aquarium with Nemo in, then you will need a test kit at some point. There are many parameters within your aquarium water that you will need to keep an eye on. Some are toxic to livestock and others need to be kept at just the right level.

If you have a basic set up that is lightly stocked and you perform regular water changes, then many of these parameters can be kept stable. However If you have a full reef aquarium with a range of corals then you might need to start 'topping up' certain parameters as the corals use them for their growth (this normally isn't something a beginner needs to worry about).

So let's briefly discuss what each of these parameters (that you will need to keep an eye on) are.

Salinity/ Density

Using your refractometer (or hydrometer, although a refractometer is much more reliable and accurate) you will need to measure the density of your saltwater water to ensure the salinity of your aquariums water mimics that found within the ocean. Salinity is basically the concentration of salt found within the water.

You are aiming for a density of around 1.025-1.026.

This parameter will fluctuate within your aquarium on a daily basis if you don't replenish the freshwater that has evaporated. The more water that evaporates, the higher the salinity level will become. The more freshwater you add the lower your salinity level will become. Whether you do this via an auto top up unit, connecting fresh water to a doser or simply add fresh water as and when it's needed this is a must for any saltwater hobbyist.

When I say fresh water, you can technically use tap water although I would not recommend it. It's always recommended to use RODI water.

Stability – Add freshwater to compensate for evaporation, test using a refractometer.

Ammonia

Ammonia is toxic to fish, corals and invertebrates. Even in low concentrations it can cause chemical burns and is lethal if the levels become high enough. The problem is that ammonia is forever being created in the home aquarium. Fish release ammonia as waste, rotting food releases ammonia as well as other forms of waste. So having a healthy biological filter that will quickly turn the dreaded ammonia into nitrate is a must.

As ammonia is so toxic it's essential that you test this parameter often in the early stages of your aquarium to ensure your biological filter is strong and healthy (as well as doing its job).

A mature reef aquarium will most likely have minimal to zero trace amounts of ammonia within the water column and many hobbyists tend to skip testing this parameter unless an issue arises. I fully recommend that you test for this parameter on a regular basis.

However in a newly set up aquarium the levels of ammonia will be high. This is of course until the nitrate cycle is complete and the bacteria (that will break down the ammonia) have started to populate the tank.

Stability – Completion of the Nitrogen Cycle. Bacteria consumes ammonia to produce nitrite. Test using an ammonia test kit.

Nitrite

So, what does ammonia become once the bacteria has a hold of it? Well the next part of the nitrate cycle is Nitrite. This parameter is also toxic to your livestock if levels get high enough. It may not be as toxic as ammonia, but you still don't want it in your aquarium.

If you are detecting Nitrite in your aquariums water then it's either a sign that there is a problem with your biological filter or an incomplete cycle in a new aquarium.

After cycling you should be reading 0 for your Nitrite tests as there should be no presence of Nitrite in your aquariums water column.

Stability – Completion of the Nitrogen Cycle. Bacteria consumes nitrite to produce nitrate. Test using a nitrite test kit.

Nitrate

So, what does Niti... yeah, I am not doing that again, you know where Nitrate comes form by now.

It's probably the safest parameter from the Nitrate cycle and it's found within every reef aquarium at some level. Although in low concentrations nitrate is next to harmless in an aquarium it can still create huge problems if the levels get to high.

You need to test for Nitrates on a regular basis (more than Nitrite and Ammonia) as you want to ensure these levels remain low. Depending on what you keep in your aquarium ultimately depends on what level Nitrate your reef tank can handle.

SPS and sensitive corals need low levels while some fish and hardier corals (like Zoa's and mushrooms) can tolerate higher levels. That been said you want to aim for a reading of 0-5 ppm, although many aquariums run with Nitrate as high as 20 ppm.

My advice is to simply keep them as low as you can.

Stability – Nitrate is produced by the nitrogen cycle and is a waste by-product. Nitrate Remover or refugium to remove nitrate. Test using a nitrate test kit.

Temperature

I don't suppose I have to go into too much detail here do I?

Simply buy an aquarium thermometer and look at it on a regular basis (once a day should do).

The problem with this parameter is that the room's temperature can have a huge effect on the overall aquarium's temperature. Checking your aquariums temperature during the summer months and hotter seasons is a must. Sudden spikes in temperature can harm livestock and if the spikes are extreme, it can be lethal.

Stability – Check thermostat daily. Check the temperature of your heater accordingly.

PH

We use the term pH to describe the acidity of the aquariums water. The pH scale ranges from 1-14. A pH reading of 7 is said to be that of freshwater, the midpoint of the scale.

Seawater has a pH of around 8.2 and therefore we aim to mimic this in our aquariums. The key isn't to get a pH of exactly 8.2, but to get it as close as we can and as stable as we can. Stability is key and is what you should aim for. A range of 7.8 – 8.4 seems to be acceptable for most hobbyists.

Any adjustments should be made gradually over the course of days/weeks as large changes can cause harm to livestock.

'Slow and Steady'

A phrase that seems to be said a lot within this hobby, and for good reason.

pH and Alkalinity are connected. The pH is stabilised by the carbonate buffers dissolved in the saltwater and the Alkalinity is the measure of these carbonates.

Stability – If to low check that your Alkalinity levels are high enough and that your water is well oxygenised. Too much carbon dioxide in the water can lower the pH. Test using a pH test kit.

Alkalinity

Alkalinity/ carbonate hardness tests are often abbreviated as KH. These tests measure the amount of carbonate and bicarbonate available in the water. Bicarbonate is a crucial aspect of coral growth so testing for this is a must.

Any adjustments to this parameter should be made gradually over the course of days. As with all parameters the key to this one is keeping it stable. Always aim for stability over the perfect reading.

If yours is lower or higher than the recommended ideal (view the parameter table) do not worry too much as long as you are able to keep it stable. If your corals and fish are all doing fine, well... if it's not broke...

Stability – Corals use this for their growth. Replace the needed amount daily by dosing an Alkalinity solution. Test for Alkalinity using an Alkalinity test kit.

Calcium

Calcium is another essential element for coral growth and health. Corals use this element to build their skeletons. If you are keeping corals then you are going to have to start testing for this on a regular basis to ensure your aquarium water has enough of this element.

If you are only keeping soft corals and fish you will most likely get by without dosing any extra calcium as your water changes will supply the aquarium with all it needs. Testing is therefore less often.

However if you have a lot of SPS or LPS corals that demand calcium for growth they may strip the water column of calcium at a much faster rate than your water changes can replenish it. Testing should therefore be carried out once per week/ bi-weekly. For this reason many hobbyists dose calcium to maintain the necessary levels. Keep in mind that sometimes when you add dissolved calcium solutions to your aquarium the pH can change, so be sure to do so slowly to avoid shocking any of your livestock.

Stability – Corals and Inverts use this for their skeleton growth. Replace the needed amount daily by dosing a Calcium solution. Test for Calcium using a Calcium test kit.

Trace Elements
Such as – Strontium, Magnesium, Iodine and Potassium

These elements are important for healthy coral growth and overall wellbeing. Only experience hobbyists tend to focus on these elements when they have a aquarium full of coral. Most beginners can simply use water changes to supply their reef with these elements. It's only when your reef begins to grow that your corals start to use up these elements faster than you can add them via water changes.

If any, the advanced beginner will often test for calcium, Alkalinity and magnesium at a push. But from experience it depends on what salt mix quality you use and what you are keeping within your aquarium to whether you need to test/dose these elements.

If you are a curious individual and love to know the inner workings of your system then there is no harm in getting the necessary test kits and becoming mad little scientists. But for the average beginner there is little need to test for these elements unless you are experiencing some issues.

Stability – Corals use trace elements for their growth. Replace the needed amounts daily by dosing a Magnesium solution and Trace Element solutions. Test for these using a specific test kit for each parameter.

Phosphate – Normally only if There is an issue.

Phosphate can often have a direct link to algae growth. It's a natural occurrence and is part of the decaying process that occurs within our aquariums.

The goal here is to keep this parameter as low as possible. Lower phosphate normally means less algae growth on your glass and within the aquarium itself.

Normally hobbyists only test for this if they have an algae issue but some simply prefer to monitor this parameter to avoid any spikes. Although it's not necessary for the beginner (If there are no issues) I recommend getting a phosphate test kit as it's always better to know your aquariums parameters.

Stability – Phosphate is a bi-product from livestock and their natural processes. You can remove this by using a Phosphate remover or by using a refugium as a natural nutrient exporting method. Test for this using a Phosphate test kit.

Copper – Normally only if There is an Issue.

Copper is commonly used as a medicine in Fish Only systems and quarantine aquariums to kill off parasites and other infections. You only really need to test for copper if you are having trouble with your inverts as copper can have a serious effect on their health.

The main reason why I mention it is that you should NEVER, yes NEVER, use copper based medicines in your display aquarium if you keep corals and inverts. Copper can leech into your rock work and stay within your aquarium for a long time to come. Like I said, copper can cause serious problems for many inverts (such as shrimps, clams and snails) and for this reason it's best not to add it to your display tank.

Stability – Copper is generally added to the aquarium as a medicine. Water changes and Carbon will remove this metal. Test for this by using a Copper test kit.

Now we know what parameters we need to keep an eye on, let's find out 'how' we do this and 'how' we maintain stable parameters!

Step 10c

How to Keep Your Parameters Stable?

Keeping your parameters stable within your aquarium is one of the most important on going tasks that you will have to manage as a reef keeper. Stability is key to a successful reef so ensuring your water parameters remain stable is a must.

Hobbyists do this in a variety of ways from using a refugium, dosing depleted elements and performing regular water changes.

The most successful and popular method for keeping parameters stable is the dosing method. Dosing is simply the process of adding elements (calcium, magnesium etc.) to your aquarium as and when your livestock consumes them. We find out how much we need to add through testing (I will go into more detail about dosing and testing later, here I simply want to explain how to you keep your parameters stable and what you will need to do).

Some of the solutions we dose are to replace used up elements and other solutions are to remove unwanted ones. There are many companies out there and most of them are widely used throughout the hobby. What you use normally comes down to two factors; personal preference and accessibility.

I will explain what I use and why, but ultimately what you decide to dose comes down to your preference and what you have access to.

Quantum

Quantum is the product that I use for all my saltwater aquarium needs. They supply all the elements that I need to dose, the salts that make up my water and the chemical filtration that I run. They are simply awesome!

So a little bit about Quantum...

Quantum have set up a four step program that is very user friendly,

Step 1 – Environmental Salts

Quantum have four types of salt that you can use to create your saltwater with. Each one has been specifically designed to suit the needs of different aquariums. All you need to do is decide what you want to keep within your aquarium and choose the salt most suited for that livestock.

For example;

I use the Mixed Macro Probiotic Salt as I have a mixed reef aquarium. This salt has been specifically designed to meet the needs of a mixed reef.

Water changes are a good method to remove and replace parameters.

Step 2 – Algae Control and Nutrient Removal

Now that you have your salt chosen for your water the second step in the Quantum program is aimed at the removal of unwanted nutrients and the control of algae. This is done via their phosphate remover, nitrate remover and their activated carbon. These are the products that we use to remove nutrients that we do not want in our aquariums.

Here is a very simply explanation of each;

Phosphate Remover
This Binds with the phosphate and allows the filters socks and filter mats to remove the bigger particles. This is the solution you will use if your phosphate levels are getting to high within your aquarium.

Nitrate Remover
The addition of a carbon source provides food (for lack of a better word I'm use the term 'food' as this is a simple explanation to give you a basis idea why we use it) for the denitrifying bacteria, the more denitrifying bacteria you have the more nitrate they consume.

Bio Active Carbon
This removes ammonia/ammonium, nitrite, odour, tannins, heavy metals & organic toxins from aquarium water. This could be the chemical filtration within your aquarium.

Tip – A refugium *will also help remove nitrate and phosphate from the aquariums water. It's a popular and natural choice of nutrient export. I personally recommend the use of both. The combination of the two will help keep your phosphate and nitrate levels very stable and low!*

Step 3 – Aragonite Enhancers

Now we have removed our unwanted nutrients it's now time to add the elements that our reef needs such as calcium, magnesium and alkalinity. All very easy to dose and all contain very clear instructions and dosing guidelines.

You use these products to maintain your calcium, alkalinity and magnesium levels by dosing the amounts that you need. These elements are used up by livestock as they grow (e.g. Corals use calcium and alkalinity to produce there skeletons) and will need topping up if they get to low.

I will go into more detail on how to dose later in this guide.

Step 4 – Bioactive Colour Intensifiers

Now that you are maintaining calcium, alkalinity & magnesium using their Step (3) Aragonite Enhancers, it is time to improve coral colouration using their Step (4) Bioactive Colour Intensifiers. These include Bio-Enhance, Bio-Gen, Bio-Kalium and Bio-Metals that provide the necessary elements along with biomolecules required for intensifying natural coral colour as well as building resistance and improving vitality.

These involve some of the trace elements that our corals need for growth and health. By dosing these solutions you are able to maintain all of your trace elements. The Bio-Enhance is a form of coral feed that aids their growth.

The above is just an example of one brand. Almost all brands follow a similar style to their stock. This just gives you an idea of what to expect from an aquarium company.

What you use to keep your parameters stable is up to you. If you prefer other companies (such as RedSea) then go with them! You will still get the results you are wanting no matter the company you go with (proving the company is trusted and has a good reputation in the hobby).

All I am doing here is making a recommendation for the company that I believe is the best in the hobby and most suited to people just starting out. If you speak to a Redsea reefer they will most likely recommend the brand they use, if you speak to a Fluval reefer, they will recommend what they use. As I am a Quantum reefer, well it's obvious what I would recommend.

The point here is there are many good brands to use and work with. Simply find one that best suits you and your reef and you are good to go.

Step 10d

Beginners Recommended Testing!

Ammonia,

Nitrite,

Nitrate,

pH,

Temperature,

Salinity,

Hardness (Alkalinity).

These are some of the basic parameters that need to be kept under control if you want to keep fish and corals healthy. If you wish to keep SPS coral or a large number of LPS coral then you will need to maintain the other parameters as well, such as Calcium, Alkalinity and Magnesium. This is normally done via dosing the correct amount of each element. If you wish to simply keep fish and a few soft coral then it's most likely that regular water changes will be sufficient.

As you are a beginner I wouldn't worry about dosing elements just yet, you will be fine with regular water changes. Worry about learning the basics firsts. There is so much a beginner has to learn so taking it slow and steady is often the best way. Once you understand the basics of parameter control and you are increasing your amount of coral in your aquarium then you can look into getting a dosing pump.

Below is a table of the parameters that need to be controlled within a saltwater aquarium. The table has the element and the recommended level it should be kept at.

TIP – Stability is key. Yes there are ideal parameters according to most but it's far better to have stable parameters over perfect ones that fluctuate.

The acceptable parameter range for a reef aquarium is an opinion rather than a clearly defined fact. Many hobbyists keep their parameters lower or higher than the 'optimal' levels and they do just fine. They do this as they aim for stability.

Stable parameters are ultimately the key, as long as you are within range of the desired levels recommended for a reef (and you are seeing no ill effect on your livestock) then chances are you are doing just fine.

Remember, every aquarium is different and each will likely run with different parameter levels.

Test	FO	FOWLR	Reef
Temperature	76-82°F	76-82°F	76-82°F
Specific Gravity (SG)	1.019-1.024	1.022-1.024	1.022-1.024
pH	7.9-8.4	7.9-8.4	8.0-8.4
Alkalinity	2.5 - 5.0ppm	2.5 - 5.0ppm	2.5 - 5.0ppm
Ammonia (NH3)	0 ppm	0 ppm	0 ppm0
Nitrite (NO2)	0 ppm	0 ppm	0 ppm
Nitrate (NO3)	<100ppm	<20ppm	<20ppm
Phosphate (PO4-3)	<5ppm	<.05ppm	<.05ppm
Calcium (Ca+2)	>300ppm	400-475 mg/l	400-475 mg/l

Step 10e

Saltwater Aquarium Maintenance

Equipment all set up and tuned to perfection, **CHECK!**

Knowledge on how to test your aquariums water parameters, **CHECK!**

Knowledge on how to keep your parameters stable, **CHECK!**

It's now time to start learning about what we need to do on a regular basis to maintain our aquariums. As stated above this is a lot easier than most think it is, the key is consistency and stability! Even when you can't be bothered you still need to perform the necessary maintenance (this is where many beginners fail).

Aquarium maintenance can generally be broken up into three stages; daily, weekly and monthly maintenance. All are just as important as the other.

Daily Maintenance

Evaporation

It doesn't matter what type or size aquarium you have, evaporation is going to happen to some degree. It's something you cannot avoid. You can minimise the rate of it, but never stop it all together.

All you need to do is add the same amount of freshwater to your aquarium at the same rate water is evaporating. Most people use an auto top off unit that supplies the aquarium with fresh water as and when it's need. Some hobbyists use a dosing pump to add fresh water throughout the day. The only issue to this method is that you have to find the correct amount of freshwater to add to your aquarium. Trial and error is normally the method for this.

But why must we add freshwater?

Well...

You must add fresh water to your saltwater aquarium to compensate for evaporation or your salinity level will rise and rise. There is no way around it. This needs to be maintained on a daily basis. Like I stated earlier, when I first started I didn't even think about evaporation. I lost my first few fish and my salinity level was around 1.038. It was a harsh lesson to learn. Nemo no.1 did not make it.

Health Checks

Now that you have livestock one of your regular tasks is to ensure your fish, corals and inverts all remain in good health.

If done on a regular basis you will get to know your fish and what their behaviour is like when they are healthy. This makes it easier to notice behavioural changes when the individual is unwell. Ideal times to perform health checks are during feeding as most the fish will be swimming around.

You want to check for a few things;

– That your fish are eating. If an individual doesn't eat for a few days don't worry. It often takes time for a fish to settle in.

– They are acting and swimming as they normally do. If the individual is normally swimming around but is hiding all the time, something might be wrong.

– Their colours are nice and bright (when fish sleep their colour often changes. This is natural and nothing to worry about).

– There are no rips or cuts on their fins or body.

– There is nothing attached to the fishes fins or body. For example, white spots or cotton wool like dots. This could indicate an infection or disease.

Unfortunately from time to time fish do die within your aquarium. If you are missing a fish and can't find it at feeding time then you best get your hands wet and try to find it, especially if it's a big fish. The last thing your aquarium needs is a dead fish decaying. This will add a huge amount of ammonia into the water column and cause problems for your other livestock.

If you do find a dead fish, I would perform a water change as soon as possible and perform some ammonia, nitrite and nitrate tests to ensure these parameters stay in check. If these parameters have spiked, then in a few days perform another water change to try to lower these levels as soon as possible.

Dosing

The term 'dosing' is a hobbyist's terminology for adding supplements (like calcium and magnesium) into our aquariums on a regular basis to maintain the waters parameters.

You can do this manually by adding the necessary amounts daily or you can us a dosing pump that will add the amounts for you. The only thing that goes into my aquarium are Quantum products. But you can use any brand as it tends to be personal choice and accessibility as to what you use.

As discussed earlier you need to maintain certain parameters within you aquarium to ensure they remain stable. To do this we test our parameters to see how much our aquarium is using up of each one daily and we add that amount daily to compensate.

To find out how much of a specific parameter your aquarium is consuming (livestock use certain parameters for growth) you need to test for that parameter over the course of a few days (normally three). Testing at the same time each day is recommended to ensure you get an accurate reading.

For example;

If Calcium is what we want to dose, we will test our Calcium levels for three consecutive days at the same time each day,

Day one – 425 ppm

Day two – 423 ppm

Day three – 419 ppm

Now we can clearly see over the course of three days our aquarium has used up 6 ppm. To find out our daily uptake of Calcium all we do is divide 6 (our uptake for the three days) by 3 (the number of days).

So from this we know that our daily uptake of Calcium is 2 ppm.

This means we simply need to dose 2 ppm of Calcium to maintain our Calcium levels within the aquarium.

All you do is simply use this method for the other parameters and you will know what amounts you need to dose daily.

Quantum products are easy to use, 1 ml of their Calcium will raise the parameter level by 1 ppm for every 100 litres. So in a 100 litre aquarium if I need to dose 2 ppm per day, I simply add 2 ml of Quantum's Calcium solution per day. Other brands will have their own measurements so check the bottle before you start dosing to ensure you are adding the right amount.

For The Beginner - Most beginners don't need to know about dosing or how to dose. I have simply mentioned it here so you have a rough of idea of how to do it if you progress in the hobby.

Temperature Checks

Temperature checks are simple and easy. All you need to do is check your aquariums thermometer. THAT'S IT! The reason I put it down as a daily maintenance task is because this is one parameter that fluctuates rapidly. A hot or cold day can have an instant effect on your aquariums temperature. So can a broken heater!

A few simple checks throughout the day can alert you if any issues start to occur and hopefully you will be able to act to prevent any loss of life. I tend to check the temperature of my aquarium most often during the summer and winter months.

If your aquarium is to cold you can always add another heater or put the heating on in the house. If your aquarium is to warm then simply place a frozen bottle of water into the sump or the display, just like an ice pack in your bait box. This way you don't add tap water to your aquarium but you do lower the temperature in your reef.

Feeding

One of the best parts in the hobby is when we get to feed our fish and Inverts! They go wild for food and it's a great time to do some health checks!

Now there are dozens of food brands on the market and to be honest most of them are good. You can feed flake, frozen, live, algae and pellet food. It comes down to personal choice and what livestock you are keeping.

I try to feed a mixture of flake, algae and frozen foods as I believe a varied diet results in healthier, more active fish. The one aspect of feeding that you need to focus on is not to over feed your aquarium. More food means more waste and more waste means more nitrate and phosphate.

Whatever you use just keep an eye how much you are feeding. Some people tend to remove the uneaten food after a length of time (3-5 minutes) but I personally leave it in as my CUC will eat whatever is left. If you do not keep a CUC then this option might be for you?

For The Beginner – Over feeding is a very common mistake made by beginners. Your fish can survive on very little food and if they are truly hungry they will hunt around the aquarium and feed on algae and small critters. If there is still left over food 20 minutes after you have fed your fish then you are feeding too much.

Quick Equipment Checks

This is just something I personally do. It is up to you if you chose to do this too as it's not normally a recommendation.

When I'm feeding the aquarium or adding supplements I tent to give the equipment a quick once over. I will check the skimmer to ensure the cup is not full and that it's working properly. I will check the wave maker and return pump to ensure there is nothing wrapped around them or clogging them up etc. I will check to make sure my filter roll mat is not stuck. Things like that are what I tend to check on.

It doesn't take long but for peace of mind I like to know that all of my equipment is doing its job.

Weekly Maintenance

Water Change

Regular water changes are fundamental to maintaining a healthy aquarium for the beginner. The volume and frequency will fluctuate for each aquarium but almost every hobbyist performs regular water changes on their system.

(The only hobbyists who do not perform water changes are those who dose the elements that they need. This is not something a beginner should be doing but I am stating it as an 'FYI' in case you hear hobbyists on social media stating they never do a water change)

Water changes are a method to remove nutrients and replenish elements. In the beginning stages of your aquarium, it may be the only way elements are replaced.

In the beginning of this guide we stated that we would cover all the simple aspect of maintaining a saltwater aquarium. This includes a brief description of how to perform a general water change.

Now I know some of you will know exactly how to do this but if this section helps just one person, to me, it was worth adding.

So, water changes...

The first thing we need to think about when performing a water change is where are you getting the water to put into the aquarium? Just like setting up your aquarium for the first time this can be done in one of two ways; mixing RO/DI water with synthetic reef salt or using natural sea water.

Refer back to *'Step 5'* to see how to mix/ obtain your saltwater. Just remember you will only need around 10-20 % of your aquariums total water volume for each water change.

Now that you have your saltwater to put into your aquarium, it's time to take some saltwater out.

Hobbyists do this in a variety of ways from taking water out of their sump to simply removing water from the display using a jug. My personal recommendation is to do it while you clean your sand bed when you are using your gravel vacuum cleaner. This way all that waste you remove from your sand bed goes straight into a bucket making your water changes more efficient.

Water changes are so easy to perform yet have a huge impact on the health of a young aquarium.

Algae

Outside of the refugium algae is a pain in the a**e!

But it can be easy to remove. If it's on the glass it can be removed using an algae scraper and if it's on the rocks or sand bed your clean-up crew will normally take care of it. Depending on the growth rate of the algae, cleaning your aquarium glass only needs to be done once a week.

Getting rid of it can be simple but it will most likely grow back within days. If you are getting algae growth in the display you ideally need to figure out why you are getting it rather than constantly removing it.

Normally this is due to high levels of nitrate and phosphate, which you would know about if you are doing regular parameters checks. See why I recommend regular parameter checks? It's to avoid issues like algae blooms as you can correct your parameter spikes as soon as they occur, which in turn prevents the algae bloom from occurring in the first place.

Evaporation

I know we have discussed evaporation in our daily maintenance section but there is one aspect of evaporation that we need to do on a weekly (or every few days) basis.

And that is...

Refilling our auto top off freshwater reservoir!

Every few days/weeks (depending on the size of your freshwater reservoir) you will need to refill your ATO water tank with RO/DI water. I keep my RO/DI water in a small 5l container so I have to refill this every few days to keep up with my aquariums evaporation rate.

How often you need to do this will depend on the size of your freshwater reservoir. I only mention this as I forgot about this once (one of my many mistakes) and my aquarium had a mini crash.

Equipment Maintenance & Cleaning

To ensure that all of our equipment is working properly some need to be check on a weekly basis. These tend to be simple 5 minute jobs but they are essential for the long term health of your reef.

Filter Socks

If you are using filter socks then they ideally need to be changed every few days.

You need to do this often as all the waste, food, fish poop and detritus the sock gathers will start to build up and rot in the aquariums water column. This is not what we want if we are trying to keep clean, stable water.

Most people have several filter socks and simply rotate the socks as they clean them.

Cleaning a filter sock is simple; you can use your shower, tap, tank water or washing machine. I personally used the shower (FYI – the family members using the same bathroom might dislike this!) and it removes all the muck from the sock. I then let it dry naturally and it's as good as new.

Skimmer Cup

How often you need to empty your skimmer cup will depend on many factors such as feeding, biomass, skimmer make etc. but it is something every hobbyist has to do. This is a smelly, nasty job but it needs doing. The last thing you want is for the cup to over flow and spill all of the 'gunk' back into the aquariums water column.

All skimmers are easy to clean as all you need to do is remove the cup from the skimmers body and rinse it under a tap. Once cleaned you simply place the cup back on the skimmer. It's that simple.

Refugium

So this might seem like a simple task but there is no harm in discussing it! On a regular basis (for me it's around once every 2-3 weeks) you will need to remove some of your algae from the refugium. This is how you manually remove organics from your aquarium. A very simple task but in order to keep a healthy refugium I believe regular 'pruning' of your algae helps with its growth and overall health.

Testing

Once a week (most people do it on a Sunday when they have some free time) you will need to perform your regular parameter tests. For this you will need your test kit and a note pad. Keeping a record of your results will give you a better understand of how your aquarium is doing. You will be able to see trends in your parameters and will easily be able to spot any issues.

As for testing you simply follow your test kits 'how to' guides. Previously in the guide we discussed water parameters and testing in detail. So if you need to recap what and why you are testing, simply go back to that section.

To make things easier I have put together a log book designed to be as easy to use as possible. This is Reef-fin's Saltwater Aquarium Maintenance Log Book. This book has everything you need to record you aquariums parameters and keep track of any noticeable fluctuations.

Monthly Maintenance

Cleaning Equipment

Cleaning equipment often gets over looked or forgotten about but it's an essential part of aquarium husbandry. It keeps the equipment performing efficiently and can also extend its life span. The deep clean only needs to be done a few times a year but makes a huge difference in the long run. Equipment isn't cheap so maintaining it (for me at least) is a must if it extends its life span.

I recommend cleaning a piece of equipment each month so you don't need to do it all at once. For example; One month you deep clean your skimmer, then the next you deep clean your return pump, then your wave maker etc. and so on and so on.

Cleaning is easy. Simply take apart the piece of equipment and wash it in tank water. For that extra deep clean you can also use white vinegar and a tooth brush. Just make sure you tell everyone you live with which tooth brush you use. From experience this can cause a huge family argument...

Chemical Media

Whatever media you use for your chemical filtration keep in mind that it will have a certain capacity (a limited amount of stuff it can remove from the water) and once this capacity has been reached the media will no longer do its job.

As a result of this the media needs to be replaced on a regular basis. For most hobbyists it's a couple of months but I personally use a small amount of carbon and replace it on a more frequent basis, normally once a month.

Most chemical media will have its lifespan on the packaging so all you need to do is make a note of when you need to change the media. Again it's a simple 5 minute job but it's one that can have huge consequences. If the media is not replaced when it's needed as everything the media has absorbed will be released into the water column.

Stock Check

I'm including this as a task even though it seems obvious. Once a month go through all of your supplements, feed, salts etc. to see if you are running low and need to go out and buy some more.

In the past I have performed a water change and removed my chemical media (carbon) only to realise I do not have any more carbon or salts to replace the amount that I have just thrown out. This is not necessarily a big issue as you can always pop to the shops the next day but it's a pain in the a**e. I'm all for an easier life and little things like that really frustrate me, hence this 'monthly task' that I now perform.

The Secret to Maintaining a Reef Tank!

If I had to state what the secret to a successful saltwater aquarium and maintenance schedule was I would have to use these four words;

Consistency,

Stability,

Patience,

and Knowledge.

If you have all four you will eventually have the reef of your dreams. You will need to CONSISTENTLY maintain your aquarium by performing daily, weekly and monthly maintenance tasks. You need to keep your water as STABLE as possible by testing you aquariums parameters on a regular basis and adding the necessary elements in the necessary volumes. You will need to be PATIENT as just like Rome, your aquarium will not be built in a day. Within this hobby nothing good happens fast and a reef takes time to mature into the beautiful systems you see on forums and google.

You will need to do research and homework to increase your KNOWLEDGE. The more you know the easier it is within this hobby to successes. Mistakes and errors tend to come from a lack of knowledge and can wipe out a reef in days.

But the biggest secret...

Learn from your Mistakes. Don't give up if something goes wrong, as most likely something will go wrong within your first year of keeping a saltwater aquarium. Not just once, but probably a few times. God knows I made many, many mistakes in my first few years.

The key isn't to avoid making the mistake in the first place but to learn from the mistake so you don't make the same one again. Mistakes are one valuable learning curve every hobbyist goes through. Learning from your mistakes improves your KNOWLEDGE and teaches you to be PATIENT. As a result of this we learn the importance of being CONSISTENT and our aquariums parameters will become STABLE.

Step 11 +

This isn't really a step like the others, as your aquarium is pretty much up and running. This is the step that every hobbyist is currently on. Those who don't follow this step tend not to last long in the hobby as they experience many mistakes and setbacks. Those who follow this step tend to get the aquarium of their dreams.

It's crucial for a successful saltwater aquarium.

And this is...

Research!

It's such a simple step, but many fail to realise its importance. You can honestly never do enough of it. Thinking of getting a new fish? Research about that fish, what it eats, size tank it needs, what its temperament is with other fish, etc. Thinking of getting a new coral? Research about that coral, what parameters it needs, how much lighting, etc. Having trouble with your aquarium? Research causes for what you have, Ask questions in forums or hobby groups, etc. or better yet simply contact us directly and we will try to help!

Within this hobby knowledge is power. It's how we overcome problems and its how we choose the ideal equipment for our livestock.

Helpful Hints

Within this section you will hear from a wide range of experienced hobbyists who have all been where you are now. I mean you must be sick of me rambling on by now?

All I did was ask each hobbyist if they could go back in time and give one tip to their past self as a beginner, what would it be?

And this is what your fellow hobbyists had to say..

Reef-fin

The biggest tip I can offer a beginner is to take things slow and do your homework. Mistakes happen when you rush into adding coral or fish before the aquarium is ready. As a result of this livestock will die and people leave the hobby as they 'can't do it'.

They can do it, they just didn't do their research and take things slow. Remember, slow and steady wins the race and Rome wasn't built in a day.

Cat

Check this reefer out on Instagram – @Takeabreakhaveakitkat_

Interact with other hobbyists on social media. For me it has been an amazing tool to learn and share knowledge and ideas with other reefers. People within this hobby are some of the nicest I have ever come across and are willing to help anyone at a moment's notice. Remember, we were once all beginners!

Research. I still do this every day, we will never know everything!

Test your water. It is so important to know your parameters. If something is out you can work on rectifying it before any problems arise. I use Aquamarine to log my results, the graph helps me to easily see any peaks or declines.

TK

Check this reefer out on Instagram – @tk.reef

Be patient, test regularly, good husbandry and regular maintenance and most importantly, don't be afraid to ask for help. There is a plethora of help out there from what I consider the most welcoming, loving community out there.

Drew

Check this reefer out on Instagram - @drewslagoon

Keep hands out of the tank as much as possible, learn from fellow reefers faults and successes and don't always try what works for others as it might not be best for your situation.

But my favourite tip, and one I believe would benefit a beginner, would have to be to have stability over trying to achieve perfect parameters.

Anthony

Check out this reefer on Instagram – @themangrovegarden

Keep it simple. Keep it stupidly simple. For success in the beginning it is best if you keep it simple and keep it basic.

When you have a good understanding of your tank (and only when) then is the time when you are ready to gradually move up to the more complex corals, fish, equipment etc. Take your time and enjoy the journey. It's definitely a journey and our reef tanks are always evolving.

Shalom

Check this reefer out on Instagram – @aquaman_shalom

After everything you read. After all the advice you received. After all the information that gets shoved in you. No one really knows your tank more than you do and only you can make it thrive.

Keefe (Shark Tank)

Check this reefer out on Instagram – @keefesreefs

The one thing I swear by (especially since starting to keep sharks) is that foot print is more important than water volume, to a sensible degree.

Sharks need room to swim and they prefer a longer, wider tank rather than a taller, slender tank. Remember to be reasonable when keeping these animals as they are predators and should be treated as such, they need room and water flow!

As you can see from the photos of their reef tanks they know what they are talking about. They were all once beginners and now they have created works of living art.

Final Note

So I know that within this book we have discussed a lot of information, equipment, livestock, etc. But I want to end on one final note that I believe is the key to success within this hobby. This is the most important piece of advice you will be given, kind of...

And that is...

IT IS YOUR AQUARIUM!

It does not belong to the guy at the pet shop, it does not belong to the loud mouth on social media (who is 'always' right) and it does not belong to me.

It is your aquarium and ultimately it should be done your way.

There is 'no one method fits all' or 'no one perfect aquarium' in this hobby. What works for one aquarium might not work for another.

You will most likely make mistakes, probably a good few mistakes (although I am willing to bet it won't be as many as I made when I firsts set up my aquarium). The key is to learn from them and not get to disheartened. If you take things slow and do your homework things will work out.

Just remember...

Don't rush,

Don't just buy on impulse or because it's nice,

Don't get hung up on the negatives, and remember to enjoy the nice little moments,

Don't be shy, ask those silly questions. It's much worse to keep them to yourself and make the mistakes!

And most importantly...

DO enjoy the journey! This is a wonderful, fulfilling, calming and beautiful hobby that has one amazing community of hobbyists.

I hope you all the best on setting up your saltwater aquarium and hopefully one day I will hear from you on our social media! It would be great to see how you are doing and how your aquarium is evolving.

This may be the end of this book but that does not mean it is the end of Reef-fin helping you out.

If you ever have a question, simply need some advice or want to show off your progress then by all means get in touch! We don't bite!

Final, Final Note!

No book is perfect, and this one is no exception. If you find errors, omissions, or anything you would like to change, please feel free to email me at reef-fin@hotmail.com

If you found this book helpful then please leave an honest review for this book on Amazon!

Honest reviews help other readers to determine whether or not this book is going to be a good fit for them. So if you have a spare 5 minutes then please do so.

Thank you for your time!

Where to Get More Information?

Thank you for taking the time to read this book.

I hope you found it helpful.

If you would like to learn more about Reef-fin, please visit our;

Facebook

https://www.facebook.com/reeffin.AquariumGuide/

Instagram

https://www.instagram.com/reef_fin/

References

Aldrich, C & Kurtz, J., (2018)
<http://www.saltwatersmarts.com> [Accessed: 29/06/2018]

Fatherree, J., (2016) Rockwork in the Reef Aquarium.
<http://www.tfhmagazine.com/saltwater-reef/feature-articles/rockwork-in-the-reef-aquarium-a-howto-guide-full.htm> [Accessed: 21/06/2018]

Fenner, R., (2001) The Conscientious Marine Aquarist: A Commonsense Handbook for Successful Saltwater Hobbyists. New Jersey: T.F.H. Publications.

Foster & Smith., (2018) Filter Media; How Mechanical, Biological and Chemical Filter Media Function. Available From: <https://www.petcoach.co/article/filter-media-how-mechanical-biological-and-chemical-filter/> [Accessed: 29/06/2018]

Foster & Smith., (2018) <www.liveaquaria.com> [Accessed: 20/06/2018]

Gripp, R., et al. (2018) <www.reefbuilders.com> [Accessed: 19/06/2018]

Hauter, D & Hauter, S., (2018) The Nitrogen Cycle. Avaliable From: https://www.thesprucepets.com/what-is-the-nitrogen-cycling-process-2924241 [Accessed: 29/06/2018]

Jones, A., (2014) So you want a Reef Tank.

Paletta, M., (2001) The New Marine Aquarium. New Jersey: T.F.H. Publications.

Reefbum (2018) Dry Rock vs Live Rock. Avaliable From: https://reefbum.com/aquascaping/dry-rock-vs-live-rock/ [Accessed: 10/06/2018]

Stan & Hauter, D., (2018) <www.thesprucepets.com> [Accessed: 21/06/2018]

Ulrich, A.B., (2014) The New Saltwater Aquarium Guide.

(2018) Top 30 Aquarium Blog sites <www.feedspot.com> [Accessed: 10/06/2018]

Images

Hesketh, J., (2018) <http://www.madhattersreef.com/types-of-saltwater-aquariums> [Accessed: 29/06/2018]

Razarami (2012) <https://www.nano-reef.com/featured/2012/razarmi-r58/> [Accessed: 06/07/2018]

(2018) <http://www.chilternaquatics.co.uk/marine/> [Accessed: 05/07/2018]

Tni.com (2014) <https://tnj.com/obama-signs-2014-tax-extenders-money-your-pocket/> [Accessed: 05/07/2018]

(2010) <https://reefbuilders.com/2010/05/26/pre-sifted-carbon-and-gfo-from-reef-scientific-are-clean-easier-to-use-media/> [Accessed: 02/07/2018]

(2012) <https://reefbuilders.com/2012/01/04/reef-dropoff-aquarium/> [Accessed: 05/07/2018]

(2013) <http://www.reefaquarium.com/2013/caulerpa-macro-algae/> [Accessed: 05/06/2018]

(2013) <https://www.reef2reef.com/ams/reverse-osmosis-and-deionization-ro-di.97/ [Accessed: 02/07/2018]

(2013) <http://www.reefcentral.com/forums/showthread.php?t=2314132> [Accessed: 02/07/2018]

(2018) <http://chucksaddiction.thefishestate.net/rock.html> [Accessed: 02/07/2018]

(2018) <http://fishkeepingadvice.com/the-nitrogen-cycle/> [Accessed: 10/07/2018]

(2018) <http://intenzeledlights.com/what-is-par-photosynthetically-active-radiation-measure-par> [Accessed: 06/07/2018]

(2018) <http://reeflabs.net/Ecotech_XR30PRO> [Accessed: 02/07/2018]

(2018) <http://www.aquacave.com/red-sea-coral-pro-salt-175-gal-mix.html> [Accessed: 10/07/2018]

(2018)
<http://www.commodityaxis.com/pumps/ViaAqua_internalpu mp.html> [Accessed: 02/07/2018]

(2018) <http://www.shovels.org.uk/bio-filter-bacteria-koi-pond-nitrifying-bacteria-enzyme-water-use-lt-extreme-winter-bacteria-500g/> [Accessed: 02/07/2018]

(2018) <http://www.sltcp.org/mangrove-restoration-tcp-sri-lanka/> [Accessed: 03/07/2018]

(2018) <http://www.ultimatereef.net/threads/aquaone-aqua-nano-30.645393/> [Accessed: 02/07/2018]

(2018) <https://blog.aquariuminfo.org/the-best-nano-reef-tanks-2018-comparison> [Accessed: 29/06/2018]

(2018) <https://modularmarine.com/collections/filter-socks-holders> [Accessed: 02/07/2018]

(2018) <https://orphek.com/amazing-japanese-reef-tank-atlantik-v4-led-lighting/> [Accessed: 02/06/2018]

(2018) <https://www.allpondsolutions.co.uk/marine-boyu-l350-tanks-upto-600l/> [Accessed: 02/07/2018]

(2018) <https://aqualabaquaria.com/products/vortech-quietdrive-wavemaker-pump-ecotech-marine> [Accessed: 02/07/2018]

(2018) <https://www.aquatix-2u.co.uk/edf120-eden-external-aquarium-filters.html> [Accessed: 02/07/2018]

(2018) <https://www.chewy.com/sunsun-submersible-500w-aquarium/dp/158814> [Accessed: 03/07/2018]

(2018) <https://www.ebay.com/p/100g-Activated-Charcoal-Carbon-for-Aquarium-Fish-Tank-Water-Purification-Filter/2282123004> [Accessed: 01/07/2018]

(2018) <https://www.iquaticsonline.co.uk/iquatics-aqualumi-t5-controller-2-x-80w-t5.html> [Accessed: 02/07/2018]

(2018) <https://www.lelong.com.my/150-200-micron-filter-socks-fish-tank-filter-evian-I5823286-2007-01-Sale-I.htm> [Accessed: 02/07/2018]

(2018) <https://www.pinterest.ca/pin/28640147609754392/>
[Accessed: 02/07/2018]

(2018)
<https://www.pinterest.co.uk/pin/385480049343826328/>
[Accessed: 02/07/2018]

(2018) <https://pixabay.com/en/wave-smashing-foam-spray-
sea-2211925/> [Accessed: 04/07/2018]

Printed in Great Britain
by Amazon

36040705R00129